A Pillow-Book

A Pillow-Book

Notes from a Reading Life

Michael O'Brien

Cairn/New York

To the memory of William Corbett (1942-2018), poet and publisher.

Copyright © 2018 The Estate of Michael O'Brien

All rights reserved

PUBLISHED BY CAIRN/NEW YORK
400 WEST 23RD ST. 6L
NEW YORK, NY 10011

ISBN: 978-1-886044-00-5

Text and cover design: Keira McGuinness

Cover art: Joan Farber

Contents

Introduction *vii*

A Note on Text and Sources *xi*

A Pillow-Book 1

Notes and Translations 171

Introduction

At the time of his death in November 2016, Michael had just begun working toward a final version of this gathering of passages from his reading and from his own letters and notebooks. He sometimes referred to it as a commonplace book, but, more often, a pillow-book. From the file he was working in ("A Pillow-Book"), he had cut a few brief entries and trimmed some longer ones that appear in an earlier draft ("Notebook"), but had not reached the point where the intended shape of this book would be readily apparent.

The question of how much Michael should be included—less Michael? no Michael?—came up from time to time in his conversation. At some stage, he wondered if the book shouldn't be more simply and genuinely a commonplace book, built almost entirely from the words of others. Perhaps he should remove, at the very least, the passages from his own letters, his reactions to his friends' books and readings. But that isn't what he decided to do in the early sections that he did manage to work on. And we should be grateful, because the entries that are pure O'Brien, or O'Brien reflecting on a quote or author, are often the equal of the quotes themselves, and sometimes surpass them. They, too, are ripe for quotation—to be stashed in our own personal commonplace books, and savored.

And what about the entries themselves? What do they take in, give back? Not surprisingly, Michael's deep love for the poets he most valued: Stevens, Williams, Oppen, Olson, Christopher Middleton, Baudelaire, and René Char among them. Their words here belong to a lifelong conversation Michael had with the great practitioners of the art of poetry and, often, the art of living—a way of being in the world. Writers he admired. Writers he wrestled with and came to terms with. Or, in the case of Pound, wrestled with and would not come to terms with. (Not on Pound's terms, anyway.) The same can be said for the entries on art, music, and movies. Further along these lines are the many passages from philosophers—Wittgenstein, Whitehead, Cavell—often focusing on the complex relationship between world and language. For Michael, those two are not interchangeable. Intertwined, yes. He cites Guillevic: "a desire to write a poetry of the actual world," and Guy Davenport: "the world is not language. A rock is not a word." I'll add: "That ball is real," what someone yelled at Michael and his friend George Quinan in an early poem of his. Michael's affinities with objectivist poetic practice extend to the conviction that the act of writing is part of the process of knowing the world, and a test of one's values.

Another story *A Pillow-Book* tells is of friendship, generosity, affection. Those, especially poets, who knew Michael as a man, will not be surprised to find that his consideration, his care, did not stop at the end of a phone call or the sign-off to an email or letter. Michael continued to think long and hard about the work of his contemporaries, his friends. And the work of younger artists, many of whom became friends as well. The readings, concerts, art exhibitions he went to, the books he was sent (or bought before being sent) often received further and closer attention in his private notebooks. The dialogue—for Michael was never comfortable with monologue—continues in *A Pillow-Book*.

More surprising, perhaps, to those who knew Michael first and foremost as a poet (a true reckoning) are the sizable number of entries about economic, political, and social matters: the omnivorous presence and baleful consequences of capitalism, the predations of unrestrained power, the cynical opportunism of politicians, the hollowing out of our public discourse, the depletion of joy. So Brecht, Adorno, Walter Benjamin, Guy Debord. But also tracings of less theoretical, more grassroots efforts to replenish the waters: Daniel Berrigan, Jane Jacobs, The Living Theatre, performance art. In addition, Michael kept entries that spoke to his outrage at specific news events—the dispiriting supporting evidence for the conceptual analyses. In the end, I think Michael felt that what we have as a bulwark against this fallen public world, is best exemplified by artists and activists whose words and deeds push back against the forces of mystification, imagining—and pressing for—as Oppen says, a "paradise of the real."

One of the first quotations Michael ever threw my way comes from Anton Webern: "To live is to defend a form." *A Pillow-Book* upholds that, honors it. Says, "This holds, this doesn't. This has value. This not. This is ground. Here. And here. In just such measure." I don't mean to make this sound like a book of solemn moralizing. Quite the opposite. It's a book of sure aim, not the sure thing. It defends the warm, capable living hand against the ever threatening dead hand, whether the latter be applied to our emotional, literary, social, political, or economic life. A book by turns contemplative, questioning, vehement, querulous, joyous, celebratory, funny. Both the raw material and the spun gold of a remarkable reader's—a remarkable writer's—life.

—Stuart Miller

A Note on Text and Sources

In editing *A Pillow-Book*, the question arose of whether to publish it largely "as is"—maintaining the format of a working writer's notebook, putting singular emphasis on the private rhythms of Michael's attention—or to enable the reader to further and more directly engage with the words that had caught Michael's attention in the first place, by citing as many of the original sources as I could find. (As is usually the case with a notebook, Michael was inconsistent in the way he noted sources, sometimes giving only an author's last name or initials, sometimes both the full name and the source, sometimes something in-between.) In the end, I chose the latter approach, making it, perhaps, a more public book than the computer draft would suggest.*

It's not possible to know for certain which entries came from the original source, which from a secondary one. As well as being an avid reader of books, Michael spent a fair amount of time reading newspapers and periodicals—particularly the *New York Times*, *Nation*, *New York Review of Books* (*NYRB*), *New Yorker*, and *London Review of Books* (*LRB*). It was often from these secondary sources that Michael drew when quoting. Quoting the quotes, so to speak. For example: Was Michael reading Kierkegaard's *Concluding Unscientific Postscript* when he plucked a quote from that text, or did he find it in John Updike's 2005 *New Yorker* review of a Kierkegaard biography, where it is neatly set off? He had only cited "Kierkegaard." Would it be better to point the reader to the Updike review or to the original work, which yielded the words that Michael wanted to preserve? It seems to me Michael's engagement here is with Kierkegaard, not Updike, so that's the source I give, realizing full well that Michael may not have read it there and, even if he had, may not have found anything surrounding it of equal interest. (Joan Farber, Michael's wife, points out, however, that he often went back to a book after seeing a quote elsewhere.) I wasn't always able to find the original source, so in those cases, the secondary source had to suffice. And, sometimes, I never found a reliable source, and had to leave only the attribution as Michael gave it.

My hope is that, in choosing this path, I haven't created an impediment to giving a true sense of the rhythms of Michael's attention. After all, the

xi

book isn't offered as a manual of style (which would make Michael cringe) but as an embodiment of Michael's profound engagement with poetry, art, music, politics, philosophy, and the physical world he inhabited with such acute regard.

—SM

*Multiple quotes from the same source are separated by a single line-space and the source is noted only following the last quote.

A Pillow-Book

Our condition surrounds us.
—David Abel

Brighter than sorrow but blue just the same
—Rachelle Garniez

Oh, qu'ils sont pittoresques les trains manqués! . . .

Oh, qu'ils sont "A bientôt! à bientôt!"
Les bateaux
Du bout de la jetée! . . .
De la jetée charpentée
Contre la mer,
Comme ma chair
Contre l'amour.★
— Jules Laforgue, *Derniers Vers*, x

She bid me take love easy
— Yeats, "Down by the Salley Gardens"

... "natural" languages always say something *more* than formalized languages can—natural languages always involve a certain amount of noise that impinges upon the essentiality of the information...
—Italo Calvino, "Exactitude,"
Six Memos for the Next Millennium

The regularly ordered state of pre-assigned functions toward which they gravitate ... does not suggest the irreversible movement into a contingent future which is the true condition of human life.
—Norbert Weiner, *The Human Use of Human Beings*

Inerte, tout brule ...★
—Stéphane Mallarmé, "L'après-midi d'un faune"

Writing wants to go on.
—Gertrude Stein

O SHIT HELL FUCK THAT WE ARE BLOCKED
in striving by what we hate
surrounding us. And do not break it in our strike
at it. The part of us
so trained to live in filth and never stir.
—Michael McClure

The cocks want to be sure of themselves.
—Jack Spicer

... in *Ferdydurke* a shameful inner world is revealed which can only be confessed to and formulated with the greatest difficulty. Yet this world is

not the Freudian world of instinct and the subconscious. It is the result of the following process: in our relations with other people we want to be cultivated, superior, mature, so we use the language of maturity and we talk about, for instance, Beauty, Goodness, Truth.... But, within our own confidential, intimate reality, we feel nothing but inadequacy, immaturity; and then our private ideals collapse, and we create a private mythology for ourselves, which is also basically a culture, but a shabby, inferior culture, degraded to the level of our own inadequacy. This world, said Bruno, is composed of the remains of the official banquet: it is as though we were simultaneously at table and under the table.
—Bruno Schulz, via Witold Gombrowicz, *A Kind of Testament*

Wearied human language
take me so that I no longer
am perpetually dispersed
and appear not to know
—Susan Howe, "Melville's Marginalia"

Blues fall'n down like hail
—Robert Johnson, "Hellhound on My Trail"

"And we just go on?"
"That's it."
"With what?"
"With nothing," he said.
—Ernest Hemingway, *Islands in the Stream*

Il se moquait de moi en me voyant étudier le grec à vingt ans;—"Vous êtes sur le champ de bataille, disait-il; c'est n'est plus le moment de polir votre fusil; il faut tirer."★
—Prosper Mérimée, *Stendhal*

... the worker's activity, reduced to a mere abstraction, is determined and regulated on all sides by the movement of the machinery, not the other way round. The knowledge that obliges the inanimate parts of the machine, through their construction, to work appropriately as an automaton, does not exist in the consciousness of the worker, but acts upon him through the machine as an alien force, as the power of the machine itself.
    —KARL MARX, *Outlines of a Critique of Political Economy*

... [the miner] forms a single body with the machine and is added to it like a supplementary gear vibrating with its incessant shaking. This machine is not modeled on human nature but rather on the nature of coal and compressed air.
    —SIMONE WEIL, quoted in Simone Pétrement, *Simone Weil: A Life*

Not to have the line that clarifies take away the vitality of the line first put down.
    —JOAN FARBER*

Pursue
lucidity that
shapely thing, you might
disappear
smelling of
straw and apples.
    —DAVID RATTRAY, "Out of the Dark"

Also there is the objectivist position. This creed is that the actual elements perceived by our senses are *in themselves* the elements of a common world; and that this world is a complex of things, including indeed our acts of cognition, but transcending them. According to this point of view the

things experienced are to be distinguished from our knowledge of them. So far as there is dependence the *things* pave the way for the *cognition*, rather than *vice versa*. But the point is that the actual things experienced enter into a common world which transcends knowledge, though it includes knowledge. The intermediate subjectivists would hold that the things experienced only indirectly enter into the common world by reason of their dependence on the subject who is cognising. The objectivist holds that the things experienced and the cognisant subject enter into the common world on equal terms.
 —Alfred North Whitehead, *Science and the Modern World*

Mallarmé's famous realization that nothing is producible of which we can say that "flower" is the name. . . . That the word, not anything the word is tied to, is the only substantiality to be discovered in a poem gave [him] ecstatic shivers; to command words' potencies was to oversee magic; to let them take the initiative was to set in motion glitterings "like a trail of fire upon precious stones."
 —Hugh Kenner

Then silence again, broken only by the sound, intricate and faint, of the body on its way.
 —Samuel Beckett, "Fizzle 1"

paradise of the real
 —George Oppen, "Some San Francisco Poems," 4

Praise what was ordered a second in the mind
 —Frank Kuenstler, "Last Poem"

Pascal arranges everything very tidily before God makes his appearance, but there must be a deeper, uneasier skepticism than that of a man cutting

himself to bits with—indeed—wonderful knives, but still, with the calm of a butcher. Whence this calm? this confidence with which the knife is wielded? Is God a theatrical triumphal chariot that (granted the toil and despair of the stagehands) is hauled onto the stage from afar by ropes?
 —KAFKA, *Diaries*, 1917

What hid will not be me if only I can touch, without breaking it, a single contour of the uncontainable.
 —CHRISTOPHER MIDDLETON, "From Earth Myriad Robed"

I could do with being restrained from inventing an opaque Liturgy. With brass mountings.
 —ROY FISHER

If we had a keen vision and feeling of all ordinary human life, it would be like hearing the grass grow and the squirrel's heart beat, and we should die of that roar which lies on the other side of silence. As it is, the quickest of us walk about well wadded with stupidity.
 —GEORGE ELIOT, *Middlemarch*

Je voudrais que mon chagrin si vieux soit comme le gravier dans la rivière: tout au fond. Mes courants n'en auraient pas souci.*
 —RENÉ CHAR, "Aromates chasseurs"

Art never seems to make me peaceful or pure. I always seem to be wrapped in the melodrama of vulgarity.
—WILLEM DE KOONING, "What Abstract Art Means to Me"

When Lady Murasaki is asked by the Prince why she writes, she says: *So there will never be a time when people don't know these things happened.*

I am not interested merely in the harpsichord as such; I feel no obligation, like the conscientious salesman of vacuum cleaners, to demonstrate all of its attachments.
    —RALPH KIRKPATRICK

The voice was the first, Furriskey was saying. The human voice. The voice was Number One. Anything that came after was only an imitation of the voice.
    —FLANN O'BRIEN, *At Swim-Two-Birds*

I said to her that beauty is a mercy. I said I don't want to argue about it.
    —BEVERLY DAHLEN

July 23. To Beaumont: it was the rector's day. It was a lovely day: shires-long of pearled cloud under cloud, with a grey stroke underneath marking each row; beautiful blushing yellow in the straw of the uncut ryefields, the wheat looking white and all the ears making a delicate and very true crisping along the top and with just enough air stirring for them to come and go gently; then there were fields reaping. All this I would have looked at again in returning but during dinner I talked too freely and unkindly and had to do penance going home. One field I saw from the balcony of the house behind an elmtree, which it threw up, like a square of pale goldleaf, as it might be, catching the light.
    —GERARD MANLEY HOPKINS, *Journals*, 1874

Ah fuck it man stories, stories, life's full of stories, they're there to help ye out, when ye're in trouble, deep shit, they come to the rescue, and one thing ye learn in life is stories, Sammy's head was fucking full of them, he had met some bastards in his time. . . .
    —JAMES KELMAN, *How Late It Was, How Late*

London, November 97. We stayed for four days in a B&B in Kilburn, which is like staying in Queens, then moved to a flat with a kitchen in South Kensington. Walked miles through the museums, without denting them: wonderful Celtic and Etruscan stuff in the British Museum, and a page of the Lindisfarne Gospels not far from a case with a draft page of *Finnegans Wake*; mind-boggling Turners at the Tate, which Joan kept going back to; Piero's *Nativity* at the National Gallery, and a haunting *St. Jerome and St. John the Baptist* by Masaccio, and Caravaggio's *Supper at Emmaus*, which I kept going back to: most often the risen Christ shows as a transfigured body, glorified, but no longer human. The Christ in the Caravaggio—like the Christ in Lawrence's *The Man Who Died*—is a human being to whom something altogether extraordinary, and terrible, has happened, and who is still trying to take it in. There was a beautiful and troubling show of James Ensor's work at the Barbican, haunted by madness (There's an engraving, *Le Pisseur*, of a man pissing against a wall, seen from the back; the wall is covered with childish drawings, and someone has written across it: "Ensor est un fou.") The Tate had no David Jones up, but as luck would have it there was a gallery show of his work, so I got to see some watercolors— landscapes and portraits—and some engravings (I'd seen his work only in reproduction, which is to say, I'd not seen it at all), and where I got condescended to more thoroughly than at any time since I applied for a job at Bard College. The gallery-owner just couldn't stop talking; he didn't go so far as to tell me that "The Rime of the Ancient Mariner" was a poem by Coleridge, but you could see he wanted to. We saw some fine theater—a version of *The Seagull* by Tom Stoppard, beautifully and touchingly played, an *Enemy of the People* with Ian McKellen that went like clockwork—and a verse play by Kenneth McLeish on the Orpheus story that should have been called *Clueless in Thrace*; you knew an Irishman had written it because there was an offstage god to rail at and an onstage cannibal mother. Heard a fine *B-minor Mass* at St. Martin-in-the-Fields, just across from the National Gallery, where the baritone soloist was in the pew in front of us. Skipped the *Sensation* show at the Royal Academy, contemporary work from the

Saatchi collection: we looked at the catalog, and it seemed so over-the-top in its chip-on-the-shoulder hostility and pugnacious outsiderdom that we decided not. (Upstairs was a show of Victorian Fairy Painting, for the faint of heart.) Looked up an old friend, not seen since 1970. Saw a wonderful show of watercolors by Charles Bartlett at the Bankside Gallery, all marsh and water and light. Henry Moore's wonderful *Locking Piece*, by the Thames just down from the Tate, a piece you just keep walking around: no aspect takes precedence, it would be impossible to photograph. Walked in various parks, including Richmond Hill, where a tame deer browsed for acorns ten feet from our bench.

March 16, '98. Hugh Seidman's new poems have a wonderful transparency; not that they're simple, but a kind of resistance in the early poems, that was the *subject* of the early poems, is gone: things are as they are, and the poems have a kind of amazed clarity, though very quiet.

Dr. Johnson enforced the strict observance of Sunday. "It should be different (he observed) from another day. People may walk, but not throw stones at birds."

According to C.E. Potter of Manchester, New Hampshire, the very word *schooner* is of New England origin, being from the Indian *schoon* or *scoot*, meaning to rush, as *Schoodic*, from *scoot* and *anke*, a place where water rushes....
—THOREAU, *Cape Cod*

Magdalena Abakanowicz's *DYBY* (1993), burlap, resin, wood, a figure seated on a wooden structure, lifesize (but the size of an adolescent), headless, armless, slender, seated on a beam, legs dangling in air, like a kid sitting on a bridge, graceful, touching, disconsolate, like an unfrocked angel. Sometimes her pieces seem formulaic (like Baskin's do), but when they work they're really something, and this one works.

A *Village Voice* reviewer [Dennis Lim] on a new-age film [*What Dreams May Come*] about how swell the afterlife is going to be: "a bottomless trough of mystic swill."

We took a whale-watching boatride in Provincetown, out to the Stellwagen Bank, which runs from 8 or 10 miles north of Provincetown almost to Cape Ann, and which is a great feeding ground for whales. Once you spot a whale, you watch it dive, then wait for it to come up, which can take some time; and to pass the time, the naturalist on board, from the Center for Coastal Studies, told us about whales' habits. At one point she said: "Sometimes the males will dive to the bottom and stay there for 30 or 40 minutes, singing the whole while." At which the lady next to me on the rail shook her head and muttered "Typical."

Marianne Moore, writing to someone [T. C. Wilson, in a letter dated September 29, 1935] who'd gotten an unexpected reaction from Ezra Pound: "It is very seldom, I think, that inferences concerning Ezra Pound can be literal ones. He has the mechanics of a somewhat rare firearm and is no two times alike."

Sunday *Times* piece on Elliott Carter: (1) *Symphonia* is performed in London because no American orchestra is willing to play it, though everybody acknowledges it's a masterpiece; (2) Boulez praising him for "refusing to compromise in a society that relentlessly pressures composers to appeal to popular taste." (3) Copland's response to the Third String Quartet: "If that is music, then I don't know what music is anymore." (4) Carter's mistrust of symphonic endings: "They always sound like a military victory, and that is not my idea of nobility."

. . . it was the first performance I had seen since I understood these things in which the actors kept still enough to give poetical writing its full

effect upon the stage. I had imagined such acting, though I had not seen it, and had once asked a dramatic company to let me rehearse them in barrels that they might forget gesture and have their minds free to think of speech for a while. The barrels, I thought, might be on casters, so that I could shove them about with a pole when the action required it. . . .
 —Yeats, "Samhain: 1902," *The Irish Dramatic Movement*

In order to film in color (which required more light), Namuth persuaded Pollock to paint outdoors. That color filming took place over several weekends in the autumn of 1950, and concluded after Thanksgiving with a sequence filmed from underneath a glass pane on which Pollock painted. At the conclusion of the filming, on a bitter cold Saturday, Pollock went straight into his house, opened a bottle of liquor, and deliberately descended into abusive, uncontrolled drunkenness for the first time in years. The anxieties surrounding the upcoming exhibition at the Betty Parsons Gallery no doubt figured in this lapse; but it has also been suggested that Pollock's recoil against the falseness of having staged for the camera a process previously private may also have spurred his self-destructive behavior.

Both of Namuth's films are being shown continuously in a viewing room adjacent to gallery fifteen. The re-created studio space can be found next to the viewing room.
 —from the leaflet for a Jackson Pollock show at the
  Museum of Modern Art, New York

It is astonishing that Alban Berg could live for years in intimate mental contact with this repulsive crew of shady derelicts and desperate clowns and crooks and care with unflagging dedication for their musical well-being.
 —Ernst Krenek, "Marginal Remarks re 'Lulu,'"
  cited in *The New Yorker*, 1981

Mrs. Berenson said Oscar Wilde was the only person of his time whose eyes did not travel on to look for someone more important when he spoke to you. She met him once five times in a week and the last time he said, "I can't possibly sit next to you, you have heard all my conversations for this week and I have nothing more prepared. Is there any one of them you would like to hear again?" "Yes, the one about Evolution," said Mrs. Berenson, and he went through it but so perfectly that it all seemed to arise from her own replies.
—CYRIL CONNOLLY, *Previous Convictions*

a gilded torrent of filth
—JACK SMITH on *Pink Flamingos*

Self-made intellectuals buy at the price of their youth what gently born and bred writers have been endowed with by nature. Write a story about a young man, the son of a serf, who had worked in a shop, been a choir boy, a high school and university student, brought up to defer to rank, to kiss the hands of priests, to submit to other peoples' ideas, offering thanks for every mouthful of bread, often whipped, going to school without shoes, fighting, torturing animals, fond of dining with rich relatives, playing the hypocrite before God and man without any cause, except out of a consciousness of his own insignificance—and tell how this young man squeezes the slave out of himself drop by drop, and how he wakes up one fine morning to realize that it was not the blood of a slave that ran in his veins, but real human blood.
—CHEKHOV, letter to A. S. Suvorin, January 7, 1889

How could they that dreaded solitude love that which solitude had made?
—YEATS, *The Irish Dramatic Movement*, of Synge and the outcry against *The Playboy*

> I may as well say what I should not otherwise have said, that I always knew in my heart Walt Whitman's mind to be more like my own than any other man's living. As he is a very great scoundrel this is not a pleasant confession.
> —GERARD MANLEY HOPKINS, letter to Robert Bridges, October 18, 1882

Provence, April '99: We stayed, a *gîte* tucked into the end of a long, one-story farm building on the outskirts of Simiane-la-Rotonde, a hill town of maybe 450 people, 10 miles north of Apt. Looking out the kitchen window in the morning, you'd see a flowering fruit-tree in the patch of earth by the side of the house; a grey dirt road; a large plowed field, planted with new lavender, the earth light brown, the furrows perpendicular to the house; green fields in the distance, a few trees along the road to the village, a grey, two-story house with its outbuildings by the road to Cheyran; the road north, to Banon; hills; beyond them, the Montagne de Lure, snow-capped; a huge sky; clouds. The weather changed all the time. The outlook was northern, a kind of rugged back-country; on a clear day you could see the beginnings of the French Alps.

It has fallen to Gustaf Sobin to take care of René Char's grave. He brought us there, a dreary necropolis in L'Isle-sur-la-Sorgue, but with words on the stone from Char's "À la santé du serpent":

> *Si nous habitons un éclair, il est le coeur de l'éternel.*★

And to some favorite 11th century churches. (I seem to like churches better with their roofs off.) And to a place on a hill outside Banon, where there's a spring that was sacred in Celto-Ligurian times, and in the Roman times that succeeded them; a healing spring, a pilgrimage site, where people would leave tiny offerings, little bronze ornaments, tiny clay votive lamps. There've been a couple of serious archaeological digs, and the site has been worked over by treasure-hunters with metal detectors, but mostly there's no one there (someone looking for firewood the day we were there). It had rained the previous day, which brings out the bronze:

Gustaf had brought tweezers for us, and a film canister into which to drop what we found in the couple of hours we spent there, before it started to thunder and it seemed prudent to get off the mountain, tiny fragments of bronze and pottery: the oldest stuff I've ever handled.

A journalist is stimulated by a deadline: he writes worse if he has time.
    —Karl Kraus

Jacob Burckhardt tells a story of a Venetian merchant who was present at one of Savonarola's Auto-da-Fés. He watched them make a great pyramid of objects to be burned: false hair and beards, scents and toilet articles, mirrors, chessboards, playing cards, lutes and harps, volumes of Latin and Italian poets, among them Petrarch and Boccaccio, and finally two tiers of paintings, chiefly of beautiful women. When the pyramid was ready, he offered 22,000 florins for the lot. The Florentines refused, commissioned his portrait to be painted on the spot, and burned it with the rest.
    —Mary McCarthy, *Venice Observed*

Asked to acknowledge the necessity for having a beginning, middle, and end in his films, Godard replied: "Certainly, but not necessarily in that order."

In my room, the world is beyond my understanding;
But when I walk I see that it consists of three or four hills and a cloud.
    —Wallace Stevens, "Of the Surface of Things"

loquitur = begins to speak (used as a stage direction)★

"Power infiltrates its zones of interest with zombies made of language—that is what clichés look like."
—CHRISTOPHER MIDDLETON, *Bolshevism in Art*

Irwin Ehrenpreis really did say, in *The New York Review of Books*, where else, that John Ashbery's poetry was more interesting to talk about than to read. This would seem to leave no one standing: it both dismisses Ashbery and explains his popularity with people who would rather talk than read.

Likeness-to-material is no more confined to direct reference (the constative poem) than sound-effects are confined to the low device of onomatopoeia. True, a poem about a basket might be made of structures that sound and feel fibrous, a poem about grass might sound grassy, have a tasseled syntax. But obliquity, the real radiance of suggestion that communicates by withholding direct reference, circling its objects without touching them, that is the gist of material correspondence.
—CHRISTOPHER MIDDLETON, "Materiality in the Poem"

Soderini was very pleased with it when it was in place. He watched Michelangelo retouch it and said he thought the nose too short. Michelangelo saw that Soderini was badly placed to view the head, but, to satisfy him, he took his chisel and a little loose marble dust in his hand and climbed the scaffolding. As he tapped lightly on the chisel, he let the marble dust drift down. "I like it better now," said Soderini, "you have given it life." Michelangelo came down, not without compassion for those who wish to appear good judges in matters about which they know nothing.
—VASARI, on Michelangelo's "David," *Lives of the Artists*

February 5, '00. The Modern has mounted its 3-panel Monet *Water Lillies* in the same room with Kandinsky's four *Panels* for Edwin Campbell (1914) and Cy Twombly's *The Four Seasons* (1993–94), and god the Twombly looks grim: shit-stained, autistic, monumentally abject. Its companions are so self-possessed, so deliberately accomplished, everything it refuses to be.

The only time I have been asked to write for the *New York Review of Books* was to review *The Country and the City*. The editors first "lost" my review for several months, then cut and copy edited it because (I was told) I had used certain terms their readers "would not understand." When the proof arrived (which I was told I must not alter), I found that the one word cut out throughout, or replaced by some euphemism, was "capitalism." I managed to get it put back once or twice, and have not been asked to write again. Raymond Williams had a way of upsetting people with overcultivated literary palates.
—E. P. THOMPSON, *The Nation*, March 5, 1988

The atoms that comprise our bodies and that make all visible stars and galaxies are mere trace-constituents of a universe whose large-scale structure is controlled by some quite different (and invisible) substance. We see, as it were, just the white foam on the wave-crests, not the massive waves themselves.
—MARTIN REES, *Just Six Numbers*

The Villa Farnesina: "a palace so splendid that the Spanish ambassador, caught in a coughing spell, spit in the face of his servant, for, he allowed later, it was the only thing of no value he could find there."

Life is a pill which none of us can bear to swallow without gilding; yet for the poor we delight in stripping it still barer, and are not ashamed to shew even visible displeasure, if ever the bitter taste is taken from their mouths.
—SAMUEL JOHNSON, in Piozzi, *Anecdotes*

In the fight between you and the world back the world.
   —KAFKA, *The Zürau Aphorisms*

Don't move from shape to shape, move through the shapes.
   —SALLY GROSS★

To live *in* the world of creation—to get into it and stay in it—to frequent it and haunt it—to *think* intently and fruitfully—to woo combinations and inspirations into being by a depth and continuity of attention and meditation—this is the only thing.
   —HENRY JAMES, notebook entry, October 23, 1891

Time is a river, the resistless flow of all created things.

Does the sun think to do the rain's work? or Asclepius that of Demeter?

You are not compelled to form any opinion about this matter before you, nor to disturb your peace of mind at all. Things in themselves have no power to extort a verdict from you.

Once you have done a man a service, what more would you have? Is it not enough to have obeyed the laws of your own nature, without expecting to be paid for it? That is like the eye demanding a reward for seeing, or the feet for walking. It is for that very purpose that they exist; and they have their due in doing what they were created to do. Similarly, a man is born for deeds of kindness. . . .

Soul of mine, will you never be good and sincere, all one, all open, visible to the beholder more clearly than even your encompassing body of flesh? Will you never taste the sweetness of a loving and affectionate heart? Will you never be filled full and unwanting; craving nothing, yearning for no creature or thing to minister to your pleasures, no prolongation of days to enjoy them, no place or country or pleasant clime or sweet human

company? When will you be content with your present state, happy in all about you, persuaded that all things are yours, that all comes from the gods, and that all is and shall be well with you, so long as it is their good pleasure and ordained by them for the safety and welfare of that perfect living Whole—so good, so just, so beautiful—which gives life to all things, upholding and enfolding them, and at their dissolution gathering them into Itself so that yet others of their kind may spring forth? Will you never be fit for such fellowship with gods and men as to have no syllable of complaint against them, and no syllable of reproach from them?
   —Marcus Aurelius, *Meditations*

I once observed mosquitoes swarming. In gray masses. Host upon host. Little creatures in a slew of other little creatures. In incessant motion. Each preoccupied with its own spoor. Each different, distinct in details of shape. A horde emitting a common sound.

Were they mosquitoes or people?

I feel overawed by quantity where counting no longer makes sense.

By unrepeatability within such a quantity. By creatures of nature gathered in herds, droves, species, in which each individual while subservient to the mass retains some distinguishing features.

A crowd of people or birds, insects or leaves, is a mysterious assemblage of variants of a certain prototype. A riddle of nature's abhorrence of exact repetition or inability to produce it. Just as the human hand cannot repeat its own gesture. I invoke this disturbing law, switching my own immobile herds into that rhythm.
   —Magdalena Abakanowicz, 1985

Nothing is a great work of art, for the production of which either rules or models can be given.
   —John Ruskin, *The Stones of Venice*

The purpose of the third way was to dismantle [the welfare state] . . . without promoting a radical response.
    —Daniel Singer, *The Nation*, November 6, 2000

If the findings are confirmed, the heart of subatomic theory, called the Standard Model, will be "insufficient to describe our universe," said Dr. Thomas B. Kirk, Brookhaven's associate director for high energy and nuclear physics.
    —*The New York Times*, February 9, 2001

We don't raise our children in isolation, but we recognize the power of the myth of redemptive violence in our society, and try to show them another way.
    —Sue Frankel-Streit, *The Catholic Worker*,
        January–February 2001

What a coward I am.
Because the rain at daybreak
beat down all the rice plants,
I work like mad,
I try to get away from the fear.
But look, again in the west
the black death floats up.
In the spring, oh in the spring,
wasn't that bright love itself?
    —Kenji Miyazawa, *Spring & Asura*, trans. Hiroaki Sato

O how lovely
The words never spoken.
    —Daniel Berrigan

G's solitude: his locatives—*under, through, towards*; not *with*.★

During the war my life was in a mess and I became a Catholic. It didn't take, and the first thing I did really after my baptism was to buy the *Collected Poems* of W. B. Yeats—like a cat looking for grass to eat.
—Kathleen Raine

Primo Levi. Who knows why he died? He died because he lost his balance. He died because it was too difficult to live. (Which is why we all die.)

By river and lakes at odds with life I journeyed, wine my freight:
Slim waists of Ch'u broke my heart, light bodies danced into my palm.
Ten years late I wake at last out of my Yang-chou dream
With nothing but the name of a drifter in the blue houses.
—Tu Mu, "Easing My Heart," trans. A. C. Graham

Dear D. [Dick Mulliken★], Just a note to say we're o.k. We were driving back from Hancock early Tuesday afternoon when we turned on the radio and learned the news. We figured there was no point in trying to get into the city, so returned to Hancock, spending the night glued to the radio. Wednesday, we drove back. From the George Washington Bridge, the skyline has a gap in it where the towers of the World Trade Center were, and a huge cloud of smoke and dust drifting east. 50,000 people worked in the towers. They estimate deaths will be in the thousands. A reporter asked Mayor Giuliani if there was an estimate of the number of dead, and he replied: "More than we can bear." 300 firemen rushed in after the first plane hit and were killed when the building collapsed. Whole engine companies are missing. Someone said the buildings went down like a house of cards, by which I think she meant they didn't fall over but collapsed into themselves. Barges are ferrying the dead across the Hudson to a makeshift morgue in New Jersey. I'm not sure why we came back; this is where we live, we couldn't bear to be away. We'll probably go back to the country on Friday, stay as long as we can. The city is ashes in the mouth.

Marianne Moore, seeing Andrés Segovia playing Boccherini on television, "his fingers moving about among the strings of the guitar like hornet legs flickering here and there over a peach to determine its sweetness."

September 20, '01. Rachelle [Garniez*]'s set last night, the band cooking, the flow of the songs, the confidence of it. All those elegies. I kept thinking about Toulouse-Lautrec: work that's harsh, truthful, observant, that never loses sight of the suffering; charged with it.

I heard Louis Zukofsky read at the embassy and hurried away afterwards not to spoil it. The partita and the Xenophanes (not previously known to me) moved me most but the main thing wasn't particular pieces, still less particular lines, although occasional twists and puns put me in a state between tears and smiles, so much as the sense of presence all through. He read without affectation and accompanying himself with a professorial patter tending to irritate, his legs a double helix under the table, turning his face this way and that in courtesy to the audience, his voice ascending to the height of the partita or the last word of the Xenophanes with absolute modest certainty. There was only one question afterward: Michael Shayer lobbed a pebble, perfect in time and aim, right in the middle of the pond, and the ripples widened out, wider and wider, till Zukofsky was stopped by some underling, the cultural attaché I presume. I didn't see Keith Owen there but, as I have said, I didn't stay to chat. I walked back through the parks—we have two together, Hyde Park and Kensington Gardens two miles or more, almost the whole length of my walk home— to keep clear of people and traffic. I was touched to know I could still, though middle-aged, not much hope left, by some stroke of luck or mark

of favour be induced to feel truths we knew when young. It made me remember things I had known and thought and pleased me that someone else should be able to make my secrets public.
    —Kenneth Cox, letter to Lorine Niedecker, quoted in her June 10, 1969, letter to the Zukofskys, *Niedecker and the Correspondence with Zukofsky*

... fanatical religious sects whose form of worship was to murder those whom they regarded as enemies of the faith.
    —Bernard Lewis, *The Crisis of Islam*

What we are up against is apocalyptic nihilism. . . . It is absurd to believe they [the terrorists] are making political demands at all. They are seeking the violent transformation of an irremediably sinful and unjust world.
    —Michael Ignatieff, *The Guardian*, September 30, 2011

I am a person who loves death.
    —Osama bin Laden, in an interview with a Pakistani journalist, reported on NPR

In Seminaries, there is a way of eating a boiled egg which reveals the progress one has made in the godly life.

[When Julien first comes to Paris, the Abbé Pirard tells him:] Do not let these Parisians hear the sound of your voice. If you utter a word, they will find a way of making you look foolish. That is their talent.

Passing unperceived owing to his lack of importance . . .

. . . a novel is a mirror carried along a high road. At one moment it reflects to your vision the azure skies, at another the mire of the puddles at your feet. And the man who carries this mirror in his pack will be accused by you of being immoral! His mirror shews the mire and you blame the mirror! Rather blame that high road upon which the puddle lies . . .

He very soon perceived that, if he were not to appear vulgar in the eyes of the Maréchale, he must above all avoid any simple or reasonable idea.

The dinner was indifferent and the conversation irritating. "It is like the table of contents of a dull book," thought Julien. "All the greatest subjects of human thought are proudly displayed in it."

He opened with a passionate impulse the *Memoirs dictated at Saint Helena* by Napoleon, and for two solid hours forced himself to read them; his eyes alone read the words, no matter, he forced himself to the task. During this strange occupation, his head and heart, rising to the level of everything that is most great, were at work without his knowledge.
—STENDHAL, *The Red and the Black*

Ignorance of fact and squeamishness of reference remain mutually supporting props of the conventional world.

... people of the half-world of talent and repute now known as the media.
—Kenneth Cox

anything shut in with you can sing
    —Ronald Johnson, quoting Gertrude Stein's
      "What Is English Literature"

Kotik's instrumental music confronts the post-Cagean problem of writing nonclimactic, uninflected music that nonetheless moves forward.
    —Richard Kostelanetz

We worked in an environment committed to neither the past nor the future. We worked, that is to say, not knowing where what we did belonged, or whether it belonged anywhere at all. What we did was not in protest against the past. To rebel against history is still to be part of it. We were simply not concerned with historical process. We were concerned with sound itself. And sound does not know its history.
    —Morton Feldman, "The Anxiety of Art"

Who cares for likeness? A likeness recognized is only something to move in from, until difference, which is identity, is found.
    —Charles Olson, "Homer and Bible"

... the border between light and dark has been lying visible to the artist on the paper before him, and rather than will it into being, his pencil has merely followed it, unpressured and unfaltering. In the nakedness of the drawing, the relaxed muscular record of the tracing hand is unmistakably different from that of the forward-groping, carving-and-correcting eyeballer, struggling with his preconceptions and expressive or idealistic yearnings.
—Julian Bell

... in a real revolution—not a simple dynastic change or a mere reform of institutions—in a real revolution the best characters do not come to the front. A violent revolution falls into the hands of narrow-minded fanatics and of tyrannical hypocrites at first. Afterwards comes the turn of all the pretentious intellectual failures of the time. Such are the chiefs and the leaders. You will notice that I have left out the mere rogues. The scrupulous and the just, the noble, humane, and devoted natures; the unselfish and the intelligent may begin a movement—but it passes away from them. They are not the leaders of a revolution. They are its victims: the victims of disgust, of disenchantment—often of remorse. Hopes grotesquely betrayed, ideals caricatured—that is the definition of revolutionary success.
—Joseph Conrad, *Under Western Eyes*

Eliot's quotations are used with extraordinary accuracy. He knows *Tristan and Isolde*, not as the man who can tell you which is the best of fifteen recordings to buy, but as someone for whom certain movements of the work say—and the same is true of his Dante and Verlaine—"Look, you are not alone in your feeling...."

Dante's Odysseus sailed after knowledge without putting his own will in order. It is the exacerbation of will and the will's attempts to do the work of imagination that make large areas of the cantos such tedious reading.

One does not, of course, undertake translation merely to show how different other cultures are, or to give barbarism an airing. The eighteenth century found Horace so appealing because of the degree of poetic civilization he represented—a fineness of balance, insight and wit that they felt to be recoverable and necessary in a civilization like that of eighteenth-century England with its own daily barbarities which needed tempering.
    —CHARLES TOMLINSON, *Poetry and Metamorphosis*
       (Clark Lectures, Cambridge, 1982)

Virtue going out of us always; the eyes grow weary
With vision but it is vision builds the eye
    —LOUIS MACNEICE, *Autumn Journal*, xvii

Whether they admit it or not, most jazz improvisers are caught within the space created by the composer of the tune they are playing. [Herbie] Nichols . . . created his own space.
    —WHITNEY BALLIETT, *Night Creature: A Journal of Jazz*, 1975–1980

What to say about Lorine Niedecker:

—something about working small;

—something about working for the page rather than the voice: that the poem is defined on the page, not in its speaking. She never gave readings.

—something about indirection, about not doing things head-on; a way of not being stupid (or obvious);

—something about a poetry that was nobody else's business.

The paving-man leans on his two-handed rammer, the reporter's
    lead flies swiftly over the note-book, the sign-painter is
    lettering with blue and gold . . .
    —Whitman, "Song of Myself," 15

With fifteen cents and that I could get a
    subway ride in New York. My heart
Is completely broken. Only an enemy
Could pick up the pieces.
"Fragments of what," the man asked, "what?"
A disordered devotion towards the real
A death note. With fifteen cents and real
Estate I could ride a subway in New York. No
Poet starved. They died of it.
    —Jack Spicer, from a notebook, 1964

L'important n'est pas de guérir, mais de bien vivre avec ses maux.*
    —L'abbé Galiani, via Ned Rorem

Duke Ellington said Mary Lou Williams is "perpetually contemporary."

Susan Butler's* show is wonderful: quiet, intricate, accomplished. The photo she used for the announcement is one of the simpler ones, actually, most of her Venice pictures involve reflections in water, wherein the normal world is dissolved and reconstituted, a shimmering, gossamer thing. She has a powerful sense of another world, or worlds, right next to this one, if only we'll pay attention. Beautiful photos of Maine, from Schoodic, black and whites, the place where water and rock meet. Still lives. A kind of deliberate eschewal of grandeur.

Sue Graham Mingus tells the story: Mingus wanted to get some people together to make an "avant-garde" record. He approached Duke Ellington, who said: "Why should we go back that far? Let's not take music back that far, Mingus. Why not just make a modern record?"

Capitalism ... is essentially psychopathic. It lives for the moment. It can plan far ahead only at the expense of its own vitality.
—NORMAN MAILER, *Harlot's Ghost*

Refreshed and clear, the moon now shines
After the fearful storm.

Now all is done,
And I can doze for a million years.

Today in flower,
Tomorrow scattered by the wind—
Such is our blossom life.
How can we think its fragrance lasts forever.
—ADMIRAL ONISHI, trans. Ivan Morris in his book
The Nobility of Failure

Is it not better, then, to be alone,
And love Earth only for its earthly sake?
—LORD BYRON, *Child Harold's Pilgrimage*

What Paul Goodman [in *Communitas*] called the attractions of urban life: pretty clothes, lipstick, crowds, privacy, bright lights.

As the story goes, a bunch of vaulting-horses, the kind gymnasts use, on the street outside a London junkshop caught Caro's eye, he took them home with him, and, one thing leading to another, ended up with *The Barbarians*, a set of seven figures, six horsemen and an oxcart, big, not quite lifesize but commanding their space, made out of ceramic and wood and iron and the vaulting-horses. At first they look like a joke, but the longer you look the better they seem. He's worked with the same ceramicist he worked with on the Trojan War pieces. The elements here seem more modular, interchangeable, tho assembled with a lovely, careful, self-generating ingenuity that wins your admiration. There are ways in which they are clumsy, but not a beginner's ways. They probably shouldn't be seen in a gallery, or not as small a one as this. (I suppose you can't leave them outside, the plush would get ruined.) Odd, compelling stuff: another purist happily going to seed.

The road, where at points the wind raised swirls of white dust without itself being felt, was as lonely as though no one had ever been along it.
—Federigo Tozzi, *Eyes Shut*, trans. Kenneth Cox

Coarse minds think all that is subtle, futile: that because it is not gross and obvious and palpable to the senses, it is therefore light and frivolous, and of no importance in the real affairs of life; thus making their own confined understandings the measure of truth, and supposing that whatever they do not distinctly perceive, is nothing.
—William Hazlitt, "Edmund Burke"

... the blind, abject admirers of power ...

... the truly melancholy part of the policy of systematically making a nation of gamesters is this: that, though all are forced to play, few can understand the game; and fewer still are in a condition to avail themselves of the knowledge. The many must be the dupes of the few who conduct the machine of these speculations.
—Edmund Burke, *Reflections on the Revolution in France*

...the homicide philanthropy of France...
—EDMUND BURKE, *Letters on a Regicide Peace*

For poetry, the perfection of language, has a special quality, which is this: it is beyond money and all its entanglements. It costs nothing to write or read and remember, belongs to everybody, can't be sold and lasts for ever...
—JAMES BUCHAN, *Frozen Desire*

Since speaking is spontaneous and latches on to all kinds of experience and structures it to our own speech forms, speech occupies the field first: The burden of proof is always on the nature of things to show that our speaking is irrelevant nonsense, rather than on ourselves to prove that it is not.
—PAUL GOODMAN, *Speaking and Language*

Open thy mouth for the dumb, in the cause of all such as are appointed to destruction.
—*Proverbs*, 31:8

If I'd have known I was going to live so long I'd have taken better care of myself.
—EUBIE BLAKE

Alexander Sokurov's *Russian Ark*: a kind of fantasia on Russian history, Russian sensibility, filmed entirely in the Hermitage Museum in St. Petersburg, in what is said to be one long, continuous, uninterrupted tracking shot, tho I realize I don't know exactly what that means (probably laying one hell of a railroad through the museum, for one thing). It's not a tour of the museum, tho some paintings are dwelt on. Re-creations of various moments in Russian history keep erupting, and the thing culminates in an early nineteenth-century ball, lovingly dwelt on and absolutely convincing, the kind of thing you've read about in Tolstoy and elsewhere but never quite got the feel of. Here you get it. And much else, your guide is a nineteenth-century diplomat, as surprised as you are to be where he is, and to be speaking intelligible Russian, but game, a wonderful character and temperament wonderfully played. It's not a movie like any other you've seen. In its dreamlike freedom of invention it's like Fellini, but the sensibility is entirely different, and it's a movie in which sensibility is everything. Tho it begins in the present, its focus is entirely before the Revolution. Was it Talleyrand who said that anyone not born before the Revolution could never understand a kind of sweetness that life might offer? So it is here.

The world has changed less since the time of Christ than it has in the last thirty years. Even after the war [of 1870], a farm in the Beauce resembled a farm of Gallo-Roman times infinitely more than that farm resembles itself today.

We are the last. Almost beyond the last. Immediately after us begins another age, a completely different world, the world of those who no longer believe in anything; those for whom this is a source of pride and glory.*
    —CHARLES PEGUY

The periwinkle, and the tough dog-fish
At eventide have got into my dish!
The great, where are they now! the great had said—
This is not seemly, bring to him instead
That which serves his and serves our dignity—
And that was done.

I am O Rahilly:
Here in a distant place I hold my tongue
Who once said all his say, when he was young!
    —EGAN O RAHILLY, trans. James Stephens

Hugh Seidman at Westbeth, March 13, 2003: He read very well, as he does, from the manuscript of a new collection. At some point he mentioned the density of the work as a difficulty; but it's not density, it's that every word counts. Nothing's wasted, nothing's in surplus. And the rhythms and cadences have that kind of spareness and economy too, so the poems bear down in an extraordinary way that requires unflagging attention. And requites it. Because the other side of that economy is an unexpected abundance, its particulars so right the art vouches for its own authenticity. I make it sound abstract, which it's not at all: human, circumstantial, touching.

Those whom we have not been able to protect are entitled to blame us for doing nothing to save them.
—ELIAS CANETTI, *The Play of the Eyes*

The word "blarney" derives from the sixteenth-century Earl of Blarney, who like other Irish chieftains at the time was asked to declare his loyalty to a foreign monarch, England's Queen Elizabeth I. He gave such a florid speech that nobody could tell whether he was submitting or rebelling.
—TERRY EAGLETON, *The Truth About the Irish*

bailotear [Spanish] = to dance a lot and ungracefully

... he always carried with him the strange image of the Cavalier, as a warning of what can happen to a man who separates his own fate from others ...
 ... he could not say it in words but only by living as he did.
—ITALO CALVINO, *The Baron in the Trees*

... the arts that have escaped best are the arts in which the public takes no interest. Poetry is an instance of what I mean. We have been able to have fine poetry in England because the public do not read it, and consequently do not influence it. The public like to insult poets because they are individual, but once they have insulted them, they leave them alone.
—OSCAR WILDE, *The Soul of Man under Socialism*

... the carnival life of the newspapers and television channels, where the population is crowned every day and told how to live.
—ANDREW O'HAGAN, *LRB*, October 9, 2003

Webern: "his pulverization of sound into a kind of luminous dust"
—VIRGIL THOMSON

The ABC of our profession is to avoid these large abstract terms in order to try to discover behind them the only concrete realities, which are human beings.
—MARC BLOCH, *Strange Defeat*

I would like to make something that is real in itself, that does not remind anyone of any other thing, and that does not have to be explained—like the letter A, for instance.
—ARTHUR DOVE

Yet Wagner was right when he spent years studying word-roots. He knew (as Charles Doughty knew) that we were coming to another of the quantitative—as against accentual—periods in culture.... (It is this question of quantity as against accent that distorts to most Scots the nature of our pibrochs of the great period. These knew no "Bar." They were *timeless* music—hence their affiliation with plainsong, with the *neuma*. Barred music—accented music—finds its ultimate form in symphony. Unbarred music—quantity music—expresses itself in pattern repetition; hence the idea that the Celt has no architectonic power, that his art is confined to niggling involutions and intricacies—yet the ultimate form here is not symphony; it is epic.)
    —HUGH MACDIARMID, "Ezra Pound," *The Company I've Kept*

I am mystified by your saying that prose fails to hold your interest. For the litterateur, prose is a step beyond poetry I feel, and then there is another poetry that is a step beyond that.
    —MARIANNE MOORE, to Yvor Winters

H.D. wanted "... a Libra wedding of St. Mark's Catholicism and Zodiac Beasts and Greek Legend, a new book of prayers for all Aquarians."
    —BARBARA GUEST, *Herself Defined*

Last verse of the *Trachiniae*: "Nothing is present here but Zeus." (Kitto, *Poiesis*). Nothing here that is not God.

What business is it of yours if I love you?
    —GOETHE

multitudes of kindled selves
—AUGUST KLEINZAHLER

Everything he knows or thinks he deposits in an encyclopedic book that he tries to keep in the form of a novel, but its structure continually changes; it comes to pieces in his hands.
—ITALO CALVINO (on Robert Musil), "Multiplicity," *Six Memos*

The great quarrel that afflicts the Nineteenth Century: the resentment of rank against merit.

I shall be a simpleton all my life, always more amazed at my own heart than at all that is happening to me.

... a Paris education prevents a person from *feeling*, perhaps, but as a compensation it teaches one to see clearly.

... one doesn't threaten to get drunk, one gets drunk. You should have sense enough to see the difference.
—STENDHAL, *The Green Huntsman*

"He is not made for this age," Lucien's father used to say to himself, "and will never be anything but an insignificant man of merit."

How heavy and sad those people are, exchanging their specious arguments which both listener and speaker know to be false! But it would shock all the proprieties of that confraternity not to exchange this counterfeit money of theirs. One has to swallow I don't know how many imbecilities, but never laugh at the fundamental verities of their religion, or all is lost.

M. Leuwen was, it is true, of an exquisite courtesy, which in the matter of his son's weakness fairly attained the sublime, and was an almost

perfect replica of reality. But Lucien had enough discernment to see that it was the sublimity of the mind, of subtlety, of the art of being polite, discreet, impeccable.
    —STENDHAL, *The Telegraph*

Mais y a-t-il une poésie *ouverte* sur le réel et une poésie fermée sur les mots?★
    —RENÉ NELLI, *Poésie ouverte poésie fermée*

God: "the Scene-shifter"

Books of natural history aim commonly to be hasty schedules, or inventories of God's property, by some clerk.
    —THOREAU, A *Week on the Concord and Merrimack Rivers*

Certainly it is hard to know what Milton thought he was doing, but I take it the man was so intensely self-assured that he hardly criticized his work—it had only to suit his feelings.
    —WILLIAM EMPSON, *The Structure of Complex Words*

In a world where books have long lost all likeness to books, the real book can no longer be one. If the invention of the printing press inaugurated the bourgeois era, the time is at hand for its repeal by the mimeograph . . .
    —THEODOR ADORNO, *Minima Moralia*

This is our entire program, which is essentially transitory. Our situations will be ephemeral, without a future: passageways.
—Guy Debord, "Report on the Construction of Situations"

Their talk . . . was reckless without hardihood, greedy without audacity, and cruel without courage; there was not an atom of foresight or of serious intention in the whole batch of them, and they did not seem aware that these things are wanted for the work of the world.
—Joseph Conrad, *Heart of Darkness*

Merleau-Ponty describes Montaigne as putting "not self-satisfied understanding but a consciousness astonished at itself at the core of human existence."

. . . we have theologized our own economic system, transforming it into something likewise rigid and tendentious and therefore always less useful to us. It is an American-style, stripped-down, low-church theology, its clergy largely self-ordained. . . . Its teachings are very, very simple: There really are free and natural markets where the optimum value of things is assigned to them; everyone must compete with everyone; the worthy will prosper and the unworthy fail; those who succeed while others fail will be made deeply and justly happy by this experience, having had no other object in life; each of us is poorer for every cent that is used toward the wealth of all of us; governments are instituted among men chiefly to interfere with the working out of these splendid principles.

Theology is written for the small community of those who would think of reading it.
—Marilynne Robinson, *The Death of Adam*

The static sense of life has disappeared along with certain universals of classical culture: the meniscus between art and life has been broken and life itself appears as a monstrous work of art, constantly destroyed and constantly renewed.

Contemporary man has inherited a nervous system which cannot tolerate the current conditions of life . . .

. . . sensual egotism builds nothing durable, but it is precisely the idea of duration that is losing credit; not to mention the idea of building . . .

Both in its internal workings and its historical development, what our Western world understands as poetry tends wholly toward a condition of pure art of which total abstraction is the unreachable outer limit.

. . . skepticism . . . can be useful as an immunizing agent . . .

. . . the poetry derived from Virgil and Petrarch which, by way of Leopardi and Baudelaire, is still the secret of the European lyric.

In Char the instant, the real moment, throws open its doors and immerses him in the concrete experience of eternity.

Solitude is difficult for poets, who are condemned to not even understand each other.
—MONTALE, *The Second Life of Art*

Everyday life, that is the Tao.
—MASTER JOSHU, in N. W. ROSS,
Buddhism: A Way of Life and Thought

Tinguely's assumption that art and life were part of a single process changed [Dieter] Roth forever.
>   —Roberta Smith, of all people, *The New York Times*,
>   March 19, 2004

Alles geben die Götter, die unendlichen,
Ihren Lieblingen ganz:
Alle Freuden, die unendlichen,
Alle Schmerzen, die unendlichen, ganz.*
>   —Goethe, in Kafka, *Diaries*, March 17, 1912

What is to be aimed at in a style is something so unobtrusive and so quiet—and so beautiful if possible—that the reader should not know he is reading, and be conscious only that he is living in the life of the book.
>   —Ford Madox Ford, "Fyodor Dostoyevsky and *The Idiot*"

O yellow head,
Crust of deception;
Pale over wheatfields, the sun.
>   —Roy Fisher, "Three Ceremonial Poems"

an old watchman of nothingness
>   —Robert Pinget, *Fable*

Teacher, if life is a graveyard to you, leave the children free to see it as a pasture.
>   —Janusz Korczak, in Betty Jean Lifton, *The King of Children*

Written into the sidewalk's wet concrete, 15th St. between Fifth Avenue and Union Square West:

> The thief left it behind:
> The moon
> At my window.*

Beauty is not like a *ne plus ultra* of what we suppose beautiful, an abstract type of the beauty before our eyes; on the contrary, it is something novel and, until life puts it before our eyes, unimaginable.

[Baudelaire] finds these unmatched phrases for all the pains, for all the balms—phrases torn up by the roots from his own heaven and hell and unfindable in any other man's, phrases from a planet which he alone has lived in and which is like nothing we know of.
—PROUST, *Contre Sainte-Beuve*

The notion of emptiness engenders compassion.
—MILAREPA

Susan Howe, talking about Wallace Stevens at Poets House, January 12, 2001: "He positions himself in the dash." (see "Autumn Refrain")

When the genocide is instead referred to as the Shoah, a Hebrew word meaning *catastrophe*, a wall is being erected against the consolations and insults of a redemptive, sacrificial theology of salvation. *Shoah*, in its biblical usage, points to the absence of God's creative hovering, the opposite of which is rendered as *ruach*. *Ruach* is the breath of God, which in Genesis drew order out of chaos. *Shoah* is its undoing.
—JAMES CARROLL, *Constantine's Sword*

[. . . a detail of the Hebrew text which has been pointed out by Robert Graves and Raphael Patai: in the second verse of Genesis, the word *ruach* in the phrase *ruach elohim* (translated as "Spirit of God" in the old version) is a feminine word.]

"Don't be no ghost, Bulworth! You've got to be a spirit! The spirit will not descend without *song*."
—from the eponymous movie

Ned Rorem: the buzz of life

. . . as the music fogs the words of a libretto
—W. S. MERWIN, "The Wake of the Blackfish"

He seemed to be no more than brushing the dust off your own ideas, settling, arranging them a little, before he gave them back to you, surprisingly luminous.
—ARTHUR SYMONS, on Mallarmé,
The Symbolist Movement in Literature

The most striking characteristic of Po Chü-i's poetry is its verbal simplicity. There is a story that he was in the habit of reading his poems to an old peasant woman and altering any expression which she could not understand.
—ARTHUR WALEY, 170 *Chinese Poems*

Armado. How hast thou purchased this experience?
Moth. By my penny of observation.
—*Love's Labor's Lost*, III, i

And the thought that he was an ordinary person and that his life was ordinary delighted him and gave him courage.
    —CHEKHOV, "The Kiss"

Bentley Layton translates *gnosis* as "acquaintance" rather than "knowledge."
    —HAROLD BLOOM, *The American Religion*

... und wozu Dichter in dürftiger Zeit?★
    —HÖLDERLIN, "Bread and Wine"

The sonnet and quatrain are like the national debt, devices for postponing the day of reckoning indefinitely.
    —KENNETH REXROTH,
        "Poetry, Regeneration, and D. H. Lawrence"

Should we distinguish two kinds of drink-offering in the poem, literal and metaphorical? Or does Pindar move so easily between them because for him the distinction is drawn far less sharply? The uses of language which we call metaphorical have been developed to span a rift that has opened up between different kinds of experience. There is much to suggest that for Pindar, who saw the city, like the family, as a growing tree, reality may have been unified to a degree we can imagine only in art (art the augury of restored wholeness, Nietzsche said), so that our distinction between letter and figure hardly holds for him.
    —D. S. CARNE-ROSS, *Pindar*

a desire to write a poetry of the actual world
    —GUILLEVIC, interview with Serge Gavronsky, *Poems & Texts*

I am not deep, but very wide, and it takes time to walk around me.
—Balzac, letter to Countess Maffei

"You have to infer the whole dragon from the parts you can see and touch," the old people would say.

They had probably left images of themselves for me to wave at and gone about their other business.

Before we can leave our parents, they stuff our heads like the suitcases which they jam-pack with homemade underwear.
—Maxine Hong Kingston, *The Woman Warrior*

Life goes on, the ordinary goes on, and yet, somewhere in the back of the mind everyone's waiting for the dirty bomb to go off, the one that fits in a suitcase and can be bought in Pakistan and will kill half a million people and make Manhattan uninhabitable for hundreds of years. A kind of latent hysteria. Which must color everything, no way it couldn't. On we go.

There are artists, [Cuthbert] Henry wrote, who make the mistake of setting up for themselves a standard of beauty. They choose to paint only those things which can be made to conform to that idea. This is the attitude of the critic and not the artist. Now if you compare this attitude with that of Degas, Manet, Monet or Pissarro, who all went to nature like children to find new beauty, and whose work points to the fact that beauty exists everywhere, then you will find that the critic leads nowhere, whereas these others are like a river carrying you to wherever you want to go.
—Esther Freud, *The Sea House*

Louis MacNeice spoke of Stephen Spender's "redeeming the world by introspection."

Feel my mind's NOT ON MY SIDE any more.
　　—Philip Larkin, letter to Kingsley Amis, September 23, 1979

... making a sort of intercalary day amid the natural darkness; not meridian dry, of course, but a soft derivative daylight, good enough for us.
　　—Walter Pater, "Duke Carl of Rosenmold"

Encore un de mes pierrots mort;
Mort d'un chronique orphelinisme;
C'était un coeur plein de dandysme
Lunaire, en un drôle de corps.*
　　—Jules Laforgue, "Locutions des Pierrots," xii

Virtue comes to Jupiter's palace to complain of her treatment at the hands of gods and men, especially Fortune. She is kept waiting a month because those inside are busy making cucumbers blossom and painting the wings of butterflies.
　　—Dosso Dossi, *Jupiter, Mercury, and Virtue*, c. 1523

Being black has taught him how to allow white people their innocence. For black people, being around white people is sometimes like taking care of babies you don't like, babies who throw up on you again and again, but whom you cannot punish, because they're babies. Eventually, you direct that anger at yourself—it has nowhere else to go.
　　—Hilton Als on Richard Pryor, *The New Yorker*,
　　　　September 13, 1999

Words that go out awry, pettishly, will return as turmoil.
　　—Confucius, *The Great Digest*

The man of breed can not be split in such a way as to be shut off and unable to rejoin himself.
—CONFUCIUS, *The Unwobbling Pivot*

bardo = the space between states of being

The frightening, constantly discussed cause of bitterness is political. Politically bitter, the person breaks out of connection with great numbers of neighbors and becomes the channel through which the political force of the world beyond enters the community to destroy its own political structure.

Life gives us little things to work on, or it gives us emptiness.

The works of art in which the community presents itself to itself sublimely ... make our job easier, and if we persist in seeing art as some strange reflection of reality, rather than as reality itself, or as something apart from life, we make things hard on ourselves.
—HENRY GLASSIE, *Passing the Time in Ballymenone*

... life is not a farce, it is "a ridiculous tragedy, which is the worst kind of composition."★
—NIGEL DENNIS, quoting Jonathan Swift, in *Swift*

Achill's mountains: Slievemore, Minaun, Croaghaun

... Mr. Shandy, the elder, who accounted for nothing like any body else ...
—LAURENCE STERNE, *A Sentimental Journey*

... its tensions [those of Hölderlin's *Andenken*] signal a defiance, a defiance of a consuming void in which foul and pure are chaotically jumbled, a void in which intelligence is stranded, a "flaming solitude / Envisioning all, without creating it." That is the void in the Mexican poet Gorostiza's devastating *Muerta sin fin* (1939), a poem which reverses almost every sign—and value—to be found in Hölderlin's.
—Christopher Middleton, *The Pursuit of the Kingfisher*

"Things and actions are what they are, and the consequences of them will be what they will be; why then should we desire to be deceived?"
—Olivier, in Julian Barnes's *Love, etc.*

For me, the anima is the part of any man that could say: I have always known I was a woman.
—D. W. Winnicott, review of Jung's *Memories, Dreams, Reflections*

... when I think that the great Bolshevik leaders proposed to *create* a free working class and that doubtless none of them—certainly not Trotsky, and I don't think Lenin either—had ever set foot inside a factory, so that they hadn't the faintest idea of the real conditions that make for servitude or freedom for the workers—well, politics appears to me a sinister farce.
—Simone Weil, letter to Albertine Thévenon (in *Seventy Letters*)

Until then my only faith had been the Stoic *amor fati* as Marcus Aurelius understood it and I had always faithfully practised it—to love the universe as one's city, one's native country, the beloved fatherland of every soul; to cherish it for its beauty, in the total integrity of the order and necessity which are its substance, and all the events that occur in it.
—Simone Weil, letter to Joë Bousquet (in *Seventy Letters*)

Poetry with mess, risk, and an ecstatic velocity, the feeling that it's all collapsing every second, up for grabs, in sheer lack of security the next word has not yet arrived.

... any disruption of Language as Usual.
    —CLARK COOLIDGE, *Sulfur* 32

... like a man who flings himself from a window and tries at the same time to reach the pavement in a graceful attitude.
    —STENDHAL, *On Love*

December 21, 1995. The anxious care I take not to wear a coat and tie: trying to keep faith with my working-class father, before he was sick. (And Fordham's rule of always wearing coat and tie: a leg up from the working class, toward the middle class and the professions.)

Information is the poetry of power, the media-based dissemblance of what is. . . . Authentic poetry [is] the free construction of everyday life.

This project (a wish for direct life) . . .
    —*Situationist International #8*

. . . things the mind already knows.
    —JASPER JOHNS

Each commodity fights for itself, cannot acknowledge the others, and aspires to impose its presence everywhere as though it were alone. The spectacle is the epic poem of this strife.
    —GUY DEBORD, *The Society of the Spectacle*

Septimus: So the Improved Newtonian Universe must cease and grow cold. Dear me.
Thomasina: Yes, we must hurry if we are going to dance.
    —TOM STOPPARD, *Arcadia*

Deja Vu Renovations

... her contempt for the self-importance of masculine public life ...
    —DINAH BURCH on Virginia Woolf, *LRB*, December 2, 2004

From the Chicago Aristotelians [Jackson] Mac Low had learned "to regard Aristotle's *Poetics* as an empirical, post-hoc analysis of two plays," not a prescriptive "recipe bk."
    —JOEL KUSZAI, *The Poetry Project Newsletter* #202

I welcome this occasion to bow once again, before I go, deep down, before his heroic work, heroic being.
    —BECKETT, "Homage to Joyce,"
        in *James Joyce: International Perspectives*

Though the Sublime of the Great Work is avoided or shunted, thanks to the melancholic doubts of old Saturn, yet the world is scratched, its startle is unthrottled, by the work of good words in order. Their play is right as the scale of their theatre or factory. Read us, they say, we are rarely and fairly compelling.
    —GERRIT LANSING, on Clark Coolidge's *Melencolia*

Tom Pickard reads with care, and with a kind of soft intensity, you'd think it would cancel itself out but it's in fact quite compelling. And he reads as if what he's doing is important, and important to get right—he glosses words as needed, starts again if a cadence goes wrong—and at the same time as if it should be clear to all of us that this isn't the greatest thing since sliced bread, or the most important thing in the world. Which, granted the level of ego around, is very appealing. The poems are militantly working class: about work, about being deprived of work. About the death of a culture. Or its murder.

... law corrupted by power perverts reason to a debased rationality in pursuit of a mechanism by which the interests of power are protected and advanced. Given a period of incubation, it metastasizes into a self-contained ideology; it becomes, as it were, a new truth. Justice and freedom are defined by it. Such are the ongoing developments of neoliberalism.
—CARMEN TROTTA, *The Catholic Worker*, January–February 2005

... he could find in himself all sorts of courage except the courage to run away.
—CONRAD, "The Planter of Malata"

... the convulsions of a world largely unaffected by the individual efforts of anyone in it
—JOAN DIDION, *Democracy*

You know very well that it is not the Tunisian grocer down the street or the Moroccan auto mechanic around the corner who threatens your identity; it is global capitalism.
—JEAN-PIERRE CHEVÈNEMENT,
former French Socialist Minister of the Interior

When I give food to the poor, they call me a saint. When I ask why the poor have no food, they call me a Communist.
—DOM HÉLDER CÂMARA

Most people go through life dreading they'll have a traumatic experience. Freaks were born with their trauma. They've already passed their test in life. They're aristocrats.
—DIANE ARBUS, in her introduction to
a MOMA monograph, *Diane Arbus*

There are no comparisons possible in the world. Everything articulates itself. In doing so it finds its own place and weight and duration and balance. All things are of like mind.
—Alan Davies

Now if we assume that abstract thought is the highest manifestation of human activity, it follows that philosophy and the philosophers proudly desert existence, leaving the rest of us to face the worst.
—Kierkegaard, *Concluding Unscientific Postscript*

I stand in awe of my body, this matter to which I am bound has become so strange to me. I fear not spirits, ghosts, of which I am one,—*that my body might*,—but I fear bodies, I tremble to meet them. What is this Titan that has possession of me? Talk of mysteries! Think of our life in nature,—daily to be shown matter, to come in contact with it,—rocks, trees, wind on our cheeks! the *solid* earth! the *actual* world! the *common sense!* Contact! Contact! *Who* are we? *where* are we?
—Thoreau, "Ktaadn"

...and
you, who live on poverty and
cannot bear to see the poor ...
—Brecht, *St. Joan of the Stockyards*

But do you think I will pray
to my own spirit against my own desire ...?
—Sorley MacLean, "Prayer"

Chris Marker, *OWLS AT NOON Prelude: The Hollow Men*. 2005. 2-channel feed on 8 monitors, 19 minute loop, sound from Toru Takemitsu's *Corona* (1962), piano Roger Woodward.

OWLS AT NOON, night birds in the day, things, objects, images that don't belong and yet are there. Leaflets, postcards, stamps, graffiti, forgotten photographs, frames stolen from continuous and senseless flow of TV stuff (what I'd call the Duchamp syndrome: once I've spotted one-fiftieth of a second that escaped everybody, including its author, this one-fiftieth of a second is mine). Bringing into the light events and people who normally remain concealed. That's more or less the project Walter Benjamin entertained in *Passagenwerk*: applying oneself to details, to tiny things scorned by historians and sociologists. It's from that raw material, the petty cash of History, that I try to extract a subjective journey through the twentieth century.

Everyone agrees that the founding moment of last century, its mint, was World War I, and that it was also the background on which T. S. Eliot wrote his beautiful and desperate poem "The Hollow Men." So the "Prelude" to this journey will be a reflection upon that poem, mixed with some images gathered from the limbos of my memory.
    —CHRIS MARKER, April 6, 2005

How this load of centuries wants to knock me down.
    —JULIA DE BURGOS, "Song of the Simple Truth,"
      trans. Jack Agüeros

a prose such as we would all gladly use if we only knew how.
    —MATTHEW ARNOLD, on Dryden, "The Study of Poetry"

the very consummation of moonstruck vanity.
    —DE QUINCEY, *Recollections of the Lake Poets*,
      summarizing an anonymous writer's view of Coleridge
      in *Blackwood's Magazine*

Christopher Ricks: "the kind of cleverness which exhausts and depletes and cannot replenish you."

These chapters are for children, and I shall try to make the words large enough to command respect.
    —Mark Twain, "How to Make History Dates Stick"

The catalogue of a picture exhibition is often very intimidating; a steady iron-hard jet of absolutely total nonsense, as if under great pressure from a hose, and recalling among human utterances only the speech of Lucky in *Waiting for Godot*, is what they play upon the spectator to make sure of keeping him cowed.
    —William Empson, "Rhythm and Imagery in English Poetry,"
        in *Argufying*

A tympany of Spaniolized bishops . . . [has] hamstrung the valour of the subject by seeking to effeminate us all at home.
    —Milton, "Of Reformation in England"

Nothing can be more contemptible than to suppose public records to be true.
    —Blake, "Annotations to 'An Apology for the Bible'"

I used to get called regularly when we lived in Jersey City (there were so many felons in Hudson County that the pool of prospective jurors was relatively small), and I never got picked, largely because most of the cases had to do with personal injury suits, and I always said that I didn't think that fairly minor injuries should be regarded as tickets to early retirement. One judge told me to stop talking immediately, before the whole panel had to be dismissed.
    —Barbara Greenberg*

We used to have a term for such artworks, which turn away from the turmoils of the world to dwell privately, exquisitely, on a sensuous pessimism. They were said to be decadent—a word that I would revive, without prejudice, for [Wong Kar-wai's] 2046, since I can think of no other way to address this secretive, intimate, gorgeous and very peculiar masterpiece.
  —STUART KLAWANS, *The Nation*, July 28, 2005

. . . our intellect would be less perfect if the mind were alone and understood nothing but itself.
  —SPINOZA, *The Ethics*, quoted in Norman O. Brown, *Apocalypse*

The deal was to make the world safe—that is, without check—for greed. But greed is paranoid, has enemies, cannot feel safe: thus its endless grievance and fury.

Translation it is that openeth the window, to let in the light, that breaketh the shell, that we may eat the kernel; that putteth aside the curtain, that we may look into the most Holy place; that removeth the cover of the well, that we may come by the water.
  —MILES SMITH, from the preface to the
  King James version of the Bible

. . . repentance from dead works, newness of life . . .
  —ditto, in ADAM NICOLSON, *God's Secretaries:*
  The Making of the King James Bible

From the shapes of men's lives imparted by the places where they have experience, good writing springs. One does not have to be uninformed, to consort with cows. One has to learn what the meaning of the local is, for universal purposes. The local is the only thing that is universal. *Vide* Juan Gris, "The only way to resemble the classics is to have no part in what we do come of them but to have it our own." The classic is the local fully realized, words marked by a place.
    —WILLIAM CARLOS WILLIAMS, "Kenneth Burke"

What John Taggart does with repetition forces the reader, sometimes against his will, to realize the poem as more than mental event. It gets the body back into it, where it belongs. Very hard to excerpt from such poems, so much are their words and phrases implicated in each other. And such drive they have, for all their circlings-back, such fierce momentum. Their power read aloud must be enormous. They are events. They make a kind of abstraction impossible.

Justine is woman as she has been until now, enslaved, miserable and less than human. Her opposite, Juliette, represents the woman whose advent he anticipated, a figure of whom minds have as yet no conception, who is rising out of mankind, who will have wings and who will renew the world
    —APOLLINAIRE in a preface to *Juliette*, via Angela Carter,
    The Sadeian Woman

started tai chi October '95

The wave is not the water. The water told you about the wave going by.
—Hugh Kenner, *Bucky*

the wallpaper of dreams
—John Ashbery, "Tide Music," *Shadow Train*

There have been souls of a heroic stamp, for whom this world seemed expressly made; as if creation had at last succeeded, for it seems to be thrown away on the saint.
—Thoreau, "Raleigh"

I continue to see them [Duchamp's readymades] in a carnival tradition as works of art for a day, which then subside into a collateral status of works in the history of art. They could be collected in an equivalent of the Smithsonian Institution. As the Smithsonian houses Lindbergh's airplane, which no longer flies, we could construct a museum of disparate objects which used to be art.
—Roger Shattuck, *NYRB*, March 27, 1997

the Museum of Former Art?

Did you catch *Britannicus* at the National Theatre of Haiti? It must be running now. Logic demands it—logic that holds a nation's classics to be a function of a nation's language. Isn't Racine just the epitome of the Haitian sensibility? Is not Racine to Haiti as Shakespeare to America?
—Lee Breuer, *Sister Susie Cinema: Collected Poems and Performances*

Next to uncertainty always put a certitude.
—Corot, to Redon

[Middleton] goes on to quote an old Eskimo poet named Orpingelik, of the Netsilik People: "Songs are thoughts that are sung out with breathing when people let themselves be moved by a great force and no longer can be satisfied with ordinary speech."
—AUGUST KLEINZAHLER, "Dance of the Intellect"

Robert Adamson's poems: his insistent refusal of transcendence. His willingness sometimes to just let a poem clank to a stop. Gorgeous in their acrid way

> . . . Outside the night
> heron swings in from the heavens,
> and cuts through the aluminium light.

and haunted by Rimbaud. His determination not to make things any better than they are, not to think poetry's meant to improve things, or improve on them. His patience.

At the beginning of *Henri Brulard* Stendhal talks of all those odious *I*'s and *Me*'s that are so embarrassing and intrusive. I agree with him. But the third person is in such cases a shabby circumvention, as if there existed a country somewhere inhabited only by Third Persons who can be summoned by proclamation to carry out brotherly services for you when you are temporarily overcome by shame.

. . . cremation, whereby the body, as a punishment because it has betrayed them, is pulverized at high speed in a macro-oven, until not a trace of their nameless lives is left.
—CEES NOOTEBOOM, *In the Dutch Mountains*

Getting agreement is not easy. The Governor and the Senate mainly represent those parts of our society that have enough wealth and power to take care of themselves; they don't need much help from the state budget. The Assembly is usually the lone fighter for working people who live in high-need school districts, and for people who need help to get health care, day care, job programs, mass transit, etc.
    —RICHARD GOTTFRIED,
       New York state assemblyman in "Albany Update"

You could never hear more finished speaking or see a finer manner; he has the hands of a hereditary royalist who never picked up a stone or touched his own shoes . . .
    —MARIANNE MOORE, on Yeats, in a letter to her brother,
       December 18, 1932

She calls her La Fontaine translation "my dubious monster."

Sex tips from Shakespeare: "One inch of delay more is a South Sea of discovery."
    —*As You Like It*, III, ii, 187

I don't know when I began it, but somehow I felt as if I had been singing it a long long time.
    —ALICE in *Through the Looking-Glass*

Joyce [to a friend, re: *Finnegans Wake*]: "Je suis au bout de l'anglais."★

Braque: "The only thing that matters in art is what cannot be explained."

True or not, the story goes that the quizzical artist Jasper Johns, visiting Beckett, showed him the drawings for *Fizzles*, their collaborative book. They were Johns's cross-hatch drawings. Each line crossing another's path. *Ad inf.* Beckett, his sight failing, took up a drawing and, holding one edge very close to one eye, peered across the surface like someone checking wood for warpage. Johns waited quietly as Beckett slowly rotated the drawing, keeping his eye close to the edge. Finally Johns broke the silence with offer of explanation. Beckett refused. "No, no," he said. "I see what you're doing. Every time it wriggles, you hit it with a brick."
—Penelope Gilliatt

From a letter to August, who characterized the tone of Roy Fisher's poems as "atrabilious": "Shorter OED says the word comes, via Latin, from Greek *melancholia*, and means just that—'melancholy; splenetic'—neither of which describes RF's poems as I know them. In both melancholy and spleen, it seems to me, spirit's been compromised, energy baffled; there's a situation in which spleen is the strongest—sometimes the only—energy available to the poem. Baudelaire sounds like this, but to my ear RF does not."

I'm never very hot on meaning. It's the sound of meaning that I like.
—Dylan Thomas

How to pronounce the name of Zukofsky's poem: "A" long, like the first letter of the alphabet, or "A" short, like the article? He means both, but how you sound it decides for one or the other. Everybody says long A, but short A, the article, does two things: it makes the title, in effect, the first line: "A / Round of fiddles playing Bach." And it makes the titles of his two longest poems—"A" and "Poem beginning 'The'"—the indefinite and definite articles.

The Spectator for May 8, 1711, in which this:

He composed an ... Epic Poem ... consisting of four and twenty Books, having entirely banished the Letter *A* from his first Book, which was called *Alpha* (as *Lucus a non lucendo*) because there was not an *Alpha* in it.

(*Lucus a non lucendo* means something like "light breaks where no sun shines." I found the thing in a *Dictionary of Latin Words and Phrases*. It sounds like the Oulipo 300 years ago, or Georges Perec's *La Disparition*. What's it called, a lipogram? I want to find out whose poem it is & what's happening: what are the other 23 books titled? does each leave out a letter?)

kith, substantive, from the Old English *cyð*, from an Old Teutonic word meaning "known," related to the Old English *cuð*, "couth": thus, 1. knowledge, information; 2. one's native land; country; 3. the persons who are known, taken collectively; one's friends, fellow countrymen, or neighbors.
So *kith and kin* = fellow countrymen and relatives.
And *couth* = known, familiar.
And *uncouth* just "unfamiliar." Well, well. God bless the O.E.D. Hard to find one's way out sometimes.

Kenneth Cox's version of Sorley MacLean's "Raasay Woods," much better—which is to say, more musical—than MacLean's own version in the *Collected Poems*—I have the sense with MacLean that all the music is in the Gaelic, that his translations intend something much more modest. Cox makes it sing. A lovely poem. I gather K.C. was good at languages: did he know Gaelic? or work from MacLean's version? I think he at least consulted it, his version sounds at times as if informed by the sense of MacLean's, which sometimes fleshes out things in the Cox—or, that puts it the wrong way: as if what underlies Cox is a sense built on both the Gaelic and English of MacLean. That it's embedded in Cox's version, tho the music's his own.

From the description of the meeting between Ulysses and Telemachus it is plain that Homer considered it quite as dreadful for relations who had long been separated to come together again as for them to separate in the first instance. And that is about true.
    —SAMUEL BUTLER, *The Notebooks*

Thinking of Swift, said Thackeray, is like thinking of an empire falling.*
    —HARRY LEVIN, *James Joyce: A Critical Introduction*

Whether a tincture of malice in our natures makes us fond of furnishing every bright idea with its reverse ...
    —SWIFT, *A Tale of a Tub*

Adorno's "Cultural Criticism and Society": What a strange piece of work, choked with rage and nausea and the kind of horrible misgiving a chess player has as he watches his opponent turn his every move against him, incorporate it into the strategy that will destroy him. The proscription of poetry seems almost incidental, certainly unexpected. He says

As a result of the social dynamic, culture becomes cultural criticism, which preserves the notion of culture while demolishing its present manifestations as mere commodities and means of brutalization.

and then, just before the prohibition of poetry

Cultural criticism finds itself faced with the final stage of the dialectic of culture and barbarism.

which would seem to pull the rug out from under the place he's just (desperately) made for himself. Writing when and where he was, a cultural critic was someone watching the end of culture, culture overcome by barbarism, or, worse, culture showing its true face to <u>be</u> barbarism, and to go on writing poems was to pretend this was not so, or not to care, or not to have all the facts.

That what Erich Heller called, with inscrutable irony, "the odyssey of *Geist*" ended in the crematoria.

That one of the lies culture told us was that this couldn't happen.

If dialectic proceeds "by a continuous unification of opposites"
and if the opposites of A's dialectic are culture and barbarism
what's their unification?
and why "the final stage"?

It is a sentence one falls into.

His airless arrogance and self-importance. Even in despair he wants to lay down the law.

"*Auschwitz*" *is both metonymy and metaphor—no? Nu?*
(Rachel Blau DuPlessis)

"metonymy" = "substitute naming"
the unspeakable name of God
"Auschwitz" a kind of speakable name for the unspeakable
but if unspeakable, no poem

In the same essay he says: "The cultural critic is not happy with civilization, to which alone he owes his discontent. He speaks as if he represents unadulterated nature or a higher historical stage. Yet he is necessarily of the same essence as that to which he fancies himself superior."

In the "Dedication" to *Minima Moralia*, he writes: "The major part of this book was written during the war, under conditions enforcing contemplation. The violence that expelled me thereby denied me full knowledge of it. I did not yet admit to myself the complicity that enfolds all those who, in face of unspeakable collective events, speak of individual matters at all."

Terry Eagleton describes him [in the *LRB*, May 28, 2006] as "a philosopher whose pessimism was more utopian than optimism because it kept faith with a suffering so unbearable that it cried out for redemption." Which leaves this unsaid: it cried out for a redemption that did not, will not, can not occur. Hard to shed the notion of redemption. Perhaps especially hard for Catholics.

[Noah Isenberg's] review of Peter Weiss's *The Aesthetics of Resistance* in *The Nation* [September 29, 2005] cited W. G. Sebald: that Weiss's work should be understood as "an expression of the *will* to be on the side of the victims at the end of time." But what if time doesn't "end" but just stops?

Michael Wood, reviewing Stanley Cavell's *Philosophy the Day after Tomorrow* (*LRB*, October 20, 2005): "Wittgenstein says: 'What we do is lead words back from their metaphysical to their everyday use.' This sounds like the whole programme of ordinary-language philosophy, but Cavell hears an entirely different, indeed contrary note in the sentence. What if the words won't come when we lead them, and why were they being used metaphysically in the first place? Wittgenstein offers, Cavell says, 'the most original philosophical account I know of how it is that we drive words away from us, into an uncontrollable structure of transcendent service.'"

Ross Feld on Philip Guston: "What if you went to the other side of the known, and instead of discovering the sublime Null, you found *something*, lots of different somethings?"

Thiefth. David Grubbs is the man's name. What I liked about it was the way in which what he'd composed was a genuine accompaniment. Too many composers just have their way with the poems they pretend to be admiring. For *Thorow* they [Grubbs and Susan Howe] sat at the same table, facing the audience, she with her manuscript, he with a laptop, which he played the way one would play a keyboard. I'd never seen anyone do that before. For *Melville's Marginalia* he moved to the piano, but there too he kept things in scale, was never overwhelming, as he easily could have been. I remember a program I heard in France, years ago, two friends, a poet and a pianist. The poet would read a couple of poems, quiet, lyrical, like Éluard. Then the pianist would play a Debussy piece. And so on. It was like watching someone be hit by a steamroller, over and over. *Thiefth* had real intimacy: a powerful sense of someone listening, and permitting us to. I'm sorry to hear she was disappointed with the performance, it seemed just right to me. Maybe we weren't demonstrative enough.

The Goldfinches of Baghdad [by Robert Adamson]. The poems invite you in. Their art is not an art of closure—they want to go on, as I wanted to go on reading them. So much world in them. The lovely, unassuming particularity of their language

> ... Outside, the river
>
> slips by; an overhanging blackbutt
> branch inscribes the surface
>
> with a line across foaming run-off.

They do not call attention to their own excellence, have a kind of transparency, their eye is on the world. As if to say, *where else would it be?* And not that they don't have insides, he's very present—the shock of the last line of the first one,

> these fragments of regret

But they have a kind of astonished wonder, and gratitude, that there's a world at all. Something other than the hell of our own insides. Something that doesn't care about all that.

Boogie woogie was the most delicate flower in the universe, and his job was to coax it into bloom.
—GEOFFREY O'BRIEN, *Sonata for Jukebox*

... his related series of novels, *Mr. Gustafsson Himself* (1971), *Woe* (1973), *Family Reunion* (1975), *Sigismund* (1977), and *The Death of the Beekeeper* (1979). Although each of these can be enjoyed alone, they are five variations on a common theme: "We begin again. We never give up."
—LARS GUSTAFSSON, "A Note on the Author," *Sigismund*

feel the whole world turning on trouble and pain
—RACHELLE GARNIEZ, "Medicine Man"

Customs are more satisfactory than laws because all the citizens or subjects of a political unit may have a hand in evolving them. Laws made by legislatures have the almost universal defect that they are inspired by the passion of property. The history of English law was for centuries a long tale of the struggle between the politicians in parliament and the juries in the courts—the politicians making laws that made a cow more valuable than the life of a man and the juries establishing customs of the courts that frustrated the politicians. You had thus Case Law, established by custom or precedent, instead of codes established on systems.
—Ford Madox Ford, *The Great Trade Route*

Stevens, "The Man with the Blue Guitar," xv:

Is this picture of Picasso's, this "hoard
Of destructions," a picture of ourselves,

Now, an image of our society?

Picasso, *Cahiers d'Art*, 1935:

... for me, a painting is a hoard of destructions [*une somme de destructions*]. I make a painting, and then I destroy it.

Stevens, "The Relations between Poetry and Painting," *The Necessary Angel* in the Vintage edition:

Does not the saying of Picasso that a picture is a horde of destructions also say that a poem is a horde of destructions?

"horde" sounds like the work of an overconfident editor. "hoard" sounds like Stevens: *somme* here = not a sum, but a gathering.

Secret agendas. The last poem in *Sleeping and Waking*, "After Hippocrates," ends

. . . Dawn has in reserve so much light,
seeping into the streets, saturating them, turning up in a place where no eye but would see.

The last phrase comes from the end of a Guillevic poem, last in a series of poems:

Tombant à pic sur un espace
Où pas un oeil ne voudra voir.

which I translated, wrongly but with great attachment to my error, as

Turning up in a space
Where no eye but would see.

Informed of my mistake by a friend who knows more French—the mistake is not an ambiguity, I just got it, diametrically, wrong—and most of the world knows more French, it would seem—I remained wedded to it, until, after some struggle, moral and otherwise, I came up with

Sheering off at a place
Where the eye shies away.

In other words. The exact opposite ones. Leaving me with this phrase in English that I liked *a lot,* and freed of the embarrassing obligation of pretending that it translated anything.

Sometimes I feel like an idiot moving baubles from one Christmas tree to another.

There is also its resonance with two lines from Stevens that have always shaken me, from the end of "Esthétique du Mal":

One might have thought of sight, but who could think
Of what it sees, for all the ill it sees.

It is a labyrinth.

The Science of Sleep is as lovely and wonderful a movie as I've seen in many, many years, tender and powerful as Jean Vigo, funny, infinitely touching, and a most powerful accession of dreamlife into a work of art. I would love to know what Ivo would make of it, and of the special effects in it, which are homemade, childish, painstaking, and utterly persuasive, at least to me. Gondry has made many MTV films, which of course I haven't seen, and probably wouldn't like, but one would have to have a heart of stone not to like this. It is both very delicate and very determined.

[Ornette Coleman] told a childhood story about his mother, who, he kept reminding me, was born on Christmas Day. After he received his first saxophone, he would go to her when he learned to play something by ear. "I'd be saying: 'Listen to this! Listen to this!'" he remembered. "You know what she'd tell me? 'Junior, I know who you are. You don't have to tell me.'"
    —BEN RATLIFF, "Seeking the Mystical Inside the Music,"
    The New York Times, September 22, 2006

This young person gave every impression of having heard there was such a thing as poetry from hearsay or report, that he had invented the music and the instrument on which it was played at the same time, so wholly unformed by reading or literary taste were these poems.
    —FRANZ BLEI in 1898, on Robert Walser, quoted by
    Michael Hofmann, *LRB,* November 16, 2006

One can follow the question of "man's relationship to nature" through an endless maze of thought and sensibilities—including man's relationship with woman as the embodiment of a nature to be subdued ...
    —Murray Bookchin, "Radical Social Ecology"

Many thanks for the [David] Schubert poems, they are first rate—more than that, far more. They are among the few poems I read that belong in the new anthology—where neither Eliot nor, I am afraid, Pound belong. I wish I could get up that anthology where the rails are polished silver they are so clear in the sunlight I should provide. There is, you know, a physically new poetry which almost no one as yet has sensed. Schubert is a nova in that sky. I hope I am not using hyperbole to excess. You know how it is when someone opens a window on a stuffy room.
    —William Carlos Williams, letter to Theodore Weiss,
        July 16, 1946

Of all possible resurrections only spring is true the rest are handmade consoling devices big organizations for our private despair much too big to be good for us.
    —Peter Schumann, *Fiddle Sermons*

All these dead people around us. Make allies of them. Active presence in the work. The transfiguration of the black text is accomplished neither by trial and error nor by science but by the projection of the devouring flame. Let them help us, all those who are alive elsewhere, let them animate the figures we've learned, inoperative without their aid.
    —Robert Pinget, *The Enemy*

To be in words is not to want. It is enough.
    —Ed Foster, "Le Cygne"

Once persuaded that I was writing my own history, I was touched by this love for a fugitive star which deserted me in the dark night of my destiny: I have wept and shuddered over these visions.
>—Gérard de Nerval, in his dedication
>(to Alexandre Dumas) of *Filles de Feu*

"So what are you going to do?"
"What I always do. Tell stories and sing."
>—Robert Ashley, *Concrete*

With the merciful You are merciful,
with the upright You are upright.
With the pure You are pure,
and with the perverse You are subtle.
>—*Psalms* 18: 26–27, Standard JPS, revised by Steve Reich

... a humility which will not allow that one can claim to be sane while living as part of such a world.
>—William Empson, on Céline, in *Some Versions of Pastoral*

L'Arbre Frappé

I
La foudre spacieuse et le feu du baiser
Charmeront mon tombeau par l'orage dressé.

II
Enlevé par l'oiseau à l'éparse douleur,
Et laissé aux forêts pour un travail d'amour.★
>—René Char

John Taggart: How different what he's presently doing seems from the poems in *Loop* and *Crosses,* in which there was a kind of block, or mass, whose engine was repetition. Things could change, struggled to, but the poems had the force and power of closed systems. And that has changed, the poems now open out, have, use, more space, more silence, more pause, more ellipsis. Or that puts it wrong. Not that matter is elided. But that they can pause. Can wait. It started with the Pastorelles, and it goes on in the new ones. They seem to have a completely different respiratory system from the older ones. They tap into the world in a different way. There's a kind of harshness that's gone. Not gone slack, just gone. Which makes room for something else. Maybe that's it: that they make room.

Nothing's faster than narcissism, which isn't going anywhere.

Thucydides said of the Athenians just before the Peloponnesian War, "They are by nature incapable of living tranquilly themselves or of allowing anyone else to do so."

So much sadness in that noise.
    —Allen Brafman*

Goya's *Asensio Julià* (1814):
"The bird a nest, the spider a web, man friendship."
    —Blake, *Proverbs of Hell*

The life I doubted all along remains, while the love we promised will not stay.
    —Daini no Sanmi (Lady Murasaki's daughter)

In short, the form of an object is a diagram of forces ...
—D'Arcy Thompson, *On Growth and Form*

... a Bolshevik, a man who dominates situations ...
—Italo Calvino, *The Path to the Spiders' Nests*

The generic we can know, but the specific eludes us.
—Gregory Bateson, *Mind and Nature*

Nothing is better for being eternal
Or more white than white that dies of a day.
—Louis Zukofsky, *"A"-12*

We must hear the music of those Braque guitars.
—Lorca, via Frank Kuenstler

Ciaran Carson reading at NYU's Ireland House on March 6th: smart, intense, almost manic, very generous as a performer. His translation of Brian Merriman's *The Midnight Court* has a wonderful, mounting, ludic energy, like Swift, like Joyce. Deirdre (his wife) was there, the reading was interspersed with some music, he on flute, she violin. I liked him enormously, I liked the way he spent himself, it was an uncommonly generous reading and talk, he was very exposed, he read the stuff as if it mattered, with passion and conviction. His intelligence was everywhere evident, likewise his sense of humor. He read two of his own poems, and a translation of a Gaelic poem that was hair-raising. *The Star Factory* seems a brilliant book to me, wonderfully inventive and self-renewing formally, and *Last Night's Fun* has the most admiring description of the institution of breakfast I ever hope to read. The Dante translation is admirable, and very funny, which doesn't happen to Dante all that often: as if the *Inferno* had been translated by Byron.

Two things his *Inferno* gets right: That Dante is terrified the whole time. And that Hell is a prison camp, run by goons and torturers.

His *First Language* is a wild book, deliberately so. There's a kind of fury of invention, led by the ear, that's like Joyce, or of which Joyce is the great exemplar. Energy enough for a dozen tired, polite, resigned books. His poems are intricate, in their hearing, in their devising, as if there were a Belfast chapter of the Oulipo—I bet he's a fan of Georges Perec. It's wonderful to watch him play with his long line, he can do anything with it, from the quiet and tenderness of "From the Welsh" to the real savagery of his Hecuba from Ovid. He's not afraid of cruelty and violence, tho they're not his stock in trade. He loves tumult, the world pouring out of Fibber McGee's closet. Wonderful things in his "Drunk Boat"—

Now see me, snarled-up in the reefs of bladder-wrack, or thrown by the waterspout like craps
Into the birdless Aether, where Royal Navy men would slag my sea-drunk corpse—

language urging itself on like a great jazz solo. He loves risk and speed and exuberance, and he seems to love his language and his world with equal ardor. How alert his poems are, and how abundant. There's a kind of fatigue, ruinous to so much work, that's just not present here. And because he places his Rimbaud in a completely foreign metric, you don't get a tired, dutiful, fourth-hand replica of how a Rimbaud poem moves, but something new to you, which means there's just a chance that Rimbaud's astonishing newness will come across.

A poem he read that night at Ireland House is in the book, a version of a poem in Irish by Seán Ó Ríordáin, "Second Nature," a poem about sorrow and sympathy, quiet and simple, full of repetition and mirroring, yet so straightforward it took my breath away when I heard it.

Perec: I don't mean that *Life* is behind *Shamrock Tea* the way the *Odyssey* is behind *Ulysses*, or *As I Lay Dying* is behind Gaddis's *Carpenter's Gothic*, a real palimpsest or tracing, but more as Schoenberg's work is behind that of later 12-tone composers, or the *Cantos* are behind Robert Duncan's *Passages* and Rachel Blau DuPlessis's *Drafts*, as instances of a method. I can imagine a framework behind *Shamrock Tea* as elaborate as the one Perec constructed for *Life*, and one the reader is to know as little about—assignments that determine just when Wittgenstein will turn up next, and what he'll be wearing. And once you start thinking this way, it changes everything: when the Jesuit motto turns up, twice, as *ad majorem Dei gloria*, do you take it as a mistake, or as a subtle feint, part of the figure in the carpet? Joyce said he wanted an ideal reader with an ideal insomnia; *Shamrock Tea* invites an ideal reader with an ideal paranoia. (As does Borges.)

Wonderful things along the way:

"They are victims of *Sehnsucht*, that Germanic yearning for a world beyond the world. I think of the ghostly whisper heard by the protagonist of Schubert's song, 'The Wanderer': *There, where you are not, only there is happiness.* For we make the stars return our gaze; we give the constellations names, that they might resemble us."

There's an astonishing violence to the poems. You're reading along, enjoying the manic, rollercoaster ingenuity, to be brought up short by your realization that what the poem is heading for is an explosion, prepared by the comparable ingenuity, and mania, of a bomber. And you remember that Carson's from Belfast. Likewise the Ovid versions, which make you realize that what's going on is not tame stuff but a horror show. That metamorphosis produces monsters. (Like the sleep of reason.) Nothing he handles is handled conventionally, everything's as if for the first time ever, he makes a dull response almost impossible. And what a gift that is.

Aidan Higgins: I read, long ago, *Langrishe, Go Down* and *Balcony of Europe*, and what I remember, vividly, is the brilliance and the nightmare depression. The death in life of the opening section of *Balcony* is as terrible and unmuted as anything I've ever read, and there's a real quality of physical dissolution, of things coming apart, in *Langrishe* that's terrifying. What saves him, and makes him readable, is the language, his love of it, his wonderfully inventive approach to it. Ciaran Carson writes about hard things, but he's not a depressive and his world is not a nightmare or a waste land.

"Elegy for My Brother": Geoffrey [O'Brien]'s wonderful poem, touching and certain in equal measure, an absolute immediacy. Such a sure use of Williams's line, making the poem, as well as elegy, a kind of homage, as if to say, "This is something Dr. Williams's invention can also do." The music seems completely unimpeded, nothing in its way, for all the bitter fact of a world that is—and crucially is not—continuous. "part / of the smoke we are becoming— / got there ahead of us". All his art, all the years of it, there, coming to bear. "the burning world / where we are poured out". Just and magnificent. Reaching back to touch his "Ghost of a Chance" from so many years ago. A poem to be proud of.

Geoffrey: It is of course very much a homage to Williams—an attempt to revert maybe to an openness that once seemed more easily available.

August: Yes, very open, emotionally frontal, full-on—moving. Brother-grief, the great rupture of connectedness . . .

The Psalms (like the Book of Job) were relentlessly Christianized by the King James translators. *Nefesh*, meaning "life breath" and, by extension, "life," was translated by Jerome in the Latin Vulgate as *anima* and then as "soul" in the K.J.V., even though, as Alter points out, soul "strongly suggests a body-soul split—with implications of an afterlife—that is alien to the Hebrew Bible and to Psalms in particular." The ancient Hebrew word for the shadowy underworld where the dead go, *Sheol*, was Christianized as "Hell," even though there is no such concept in the Hebrew Bible. Alter prefers the words "victory" and "rescue" as translations of *yeshu'ah*, and eschews the Christian version, which is the heavily loaded "salvation." . . . Suddenly, in a world without Heaven, Hell, the soul, and eternal salvation or redemption, the theological stakes seem more local and temporal: "So teach us to number our days."
  —JAMES WOOD, reviewing Robert Alter's
    Book of Psalms in *The New Yorker*, October 1, 2007

A while ago there opened on 23rd St. between 8th and 9th a hole-in-the-wall store that called itself "Choux Factory," which was Japanese-run and sold creampuffs. (I'm not making this up.) It looked for a long time as if they weren't doing so well—people didn't get the pun, or thought it was stupid, or thought "choux" meant "cabbage" and what the hell were they talking about, or didn't like their creampuffs. Whatever. Today I noticed that, as if in explanation, just below "Choux Factory" in their window there was a smaller sign, which read: "Atelier de Cream Puff."

Notice in the *Times* for a White Elephant Sale at the New York Theosophical Society.

. . . Cheney's historically unsubstantiated conviction that violence, if violent enough, invariably generates compliance . . .
    —STEPHEN HOLMES reviewing Chalmers Johnson's *Nemesis* in *The Nation*, October 29, 2007

Whatever the hands of man take up with love is holy. (2 Aug. 42)

I must make up my mind to this once and for all: seriousness and politics are two perfectly separate things. (18 Nov. 42)

You ought to leave all this behind—consorting with felons and idiots, helping out—not so as to be able to do something else, or to devote yourself to literature, but to empty your life, to straighten it out. (1 Aug. 43)

The sea empty, without furniture, like a house with four bare walls. (11 Oct. 43)

. . . the astonishing shadow of that tree yesterday. (4 July 53)

the dervishes (6 Dec. 53)

Tradition like a wave, stronger than humans themselves, and nothing else has any meaning any more: not the skulduggery and simony of the monks, nor the ironmongery and planks that hold up the church, not even the terrible bad taste that marks every aspect of the ritual. (17 April 54)
    —GEORGE SEFERIS, *A Levant Journal*

in the stone's despair the eroded power
    —SEFERIS, "Engomi"

All poems written or unwritten exist. I don't mean a Platonic but a biological existence. Their relation to their written form is the relation of the model to its portrait. The special ability of the poet is to see them: that's why the poets are sometimes called seers.

The faculty of seeing them makes the poet, the faculty of painting (i.e., writing) them makes the talent of the poet. That's why we may have (and had) poets without talent; but mere talent without the poetical gift (i.e., the gift of the seer) is inconceivable.

Poems do not live alone. . . .
—SEFERIS, writing in English, *Personal Landscape*, 1944

Reading the *Cantos* always felt like failing a test, a test I could only pass by becoming Ezra Pound, and one seemed enough.

The Cantos. A poem without a title.

I am reminded of a statement made by Donella Meadows at a Dartmouth teach-in. She explained that there was alternative energy for everything in normal comfortable American life—television, air conditioners, light, heat, cars. There was only one enterprise that required such massive infusion of energy for which no alternative to oil could work—and that was war. A tank, she said, could move only seventeen feet on a gallon of gasoline. So this is the final purpose. This has been a war to maintain turmoil in the world (particularly in the Middle East). This has been a war to ensure that Americans can continue to make war, and like it.
—GRACE PALEY, "The Gulf War"

smart, greedy madmen
—GRACE PALEY

Ben Jonson calls Machiavelli "Saint Nicholas."

insatiable addiction to power
—Jane Jacobs

The "education of princes" ends with Pound presenting *A Draft of XXX Cantos* to Mussolini.

... his astonishing sympathy for powerless dreamers, especially when they came dressed up and ready to kill or were full of hidden erotic hope.
—Colm Tóibín, on Tennessee Williams,
in *New Ways to Kill Your Mother*

La Belle Epoque Tango Club at the Ukrainian East Village Restaurant

Frank Kuenstler's poems: joy at the level of language

Would we believe in the words of love if they did not carry the hope of that union of the real and the imaginary of which the lovers' encounter forms the allegory?
—André Breton, "Inquiry into Erotic Representations"

The Israeli government claims that they are obliged to take these measures to combat terrorism. The claim is a feint. The true aim of the stranglehold is to destroy the indigenous population's sense of temporal and spatial continuity so that they either leave or become indentured servants. And it's here that the dead help the living to resist. It's here that men and women make their decisions to become martyrs. The stranglehold inspires the terrorism it purports to be fighting.
—John Berger, "Stones"

There's an ad papering the city for a new TV series, named for its main character, who is described as "America's Favorite Serial Killer" (I'm not making this up): huge picture of some actor's head, stupid, you'd say, except more guarded than that, careful that no intelligence should show, a kind of curdled boyish charm, cheek flecked with blood lest you should fail to get the picture. Back from a hard day's work at Abu Ghraib. I'm amazed no one has pointed out the resemblance to Bush. What a sick country.

You say of Ashbery: "He is interested in how the intelligible confounds us." Does this really mean "in how the intelligible confounds us," or just "that the intelligible confounds us"? If the former, then *how*? How *does* the intelligible confound us? Or is there imprecision here, a kind of slippage from reading Ashbery, who despairs of meaning, who has thrown up his hands? We used to think of despair as a kind of anguish, but there are versions of it that are total, frictionless, without affect, almost pleasant. So here. It is bad for clarity. What is there to be clear about? And with what? are fair questions, but not nonsense, and not addressed by a poetry of programmatic evasion and inconsequence, open to everything except meaning, from which it pretends to rescue us.
 —from a letter [from Michael] to Adam Phillips

What time is it, my mother asked. 7:30, I answered. My mother nodded slowly two or three times, incorporating 7:30 into something she was working out in her mind. What time is it here, she asked.
 —ALLEN BRAFMAN

Thinking about Creeley. The first chapter of Hemingway's posthumous *The Gates of Eden* is exemplary of a double thing that goes on in his writing, a foreground entirely determined by the desire to live in sensation alone—Keats's "O for a life of Sensations rather than of Thoughts!"—and a pervasive background anxiety that stems from knowing one cannot. Creeley reverses the terms, sensation entirely in the background, the foreground taken up by the anxiety. At best his rhythmic sense was so precise, so particular to its occasion, that it made you overlook how generic what he noticed could be, saved from dullness, animated, only by his anxieties, their constancy and his constancy to them.

The extreme Tories, who wanted a quarrel with the United States; the reckless, who were delighted with every act of violence, which they called energy; the mountebanks, represented by Cobbett, who talked at random according to personal prejudices . . .

History has nothing to do with law except to record the development of legal principles. The question whether the embargo was or was not Constitutional depended for an answer on the decision of Congress, President, and Judiciary, and the assent of the States. Whatever unanimous decision these political bodies might make, no matter how extravagant, was law until it should be reversed.

Dull, obstinate, sullen, just shrewd enough to be suspicious, and with just enough passion to make him vindictive, Ferdinand was destined to become the last and worst of the Spanish Bourbon kings . . .

Probably at least five thousand families of working-men were reduced to pauperism by the embargo and the decrees of Napoleon; but these sufferers, who possessed not a vote among them and had been in no way party to the acts of either government, were the only real friends whom Jefferson could hope to find among the people of England; and his embargo ground them in the dust in order to fatten the squires and ship-owners who had devised the Orders in Council. If the English laborers rioted, they were shot: if the West Indian slaves could not be fed, they died. The embargo served only to lower the wages and the moral standard of the laboring classes throughout the British empire, and to prove their helplessness.

Flattery like this was rare in Pickering's toilsome career; and man, almost in the full degree of his antipathy to demagogy, yearns for the popular regard he will not seek.

That this strong, self-asserting Boston gentleman, gifted, ambitious, the embodiment of Massachusetts traditions and British prejudices, should feel deep contempt for the moral courage and the understanding of men whose motives were beyond the range of his sympathies and experience, was natural; for Josiah Quincy belonged to a class of Americans who cared so intensely for their own convictions that they could not care for a nation which did not represent them; and in his eyes Jefferson was a transparent fraud, his followers were dupes or ruffians, and the nation was hastening to a fatal crisis.
    —Henry Adams, *Second Administration of Jefferson*

[Ed] Barrett's *Bosston*: he makes it out of the languages around him, some of them poisoned, using them all with equanimity, in the freest way, democratic as Whitman or Mabou Mines or the *National Enquirer*, as if purity were an outrageous imposture, "A loud flailing in answer to dreams of permanence," yet without satire, never superior to his material, full of rebar, a word he likes, sometimes very moving, as in the first of the poems in the section called "John Wieners at Filene's," all of it sounding like something someone in a bar is telling you with dispassionate insistence, straight from the horse's mouth.

Anything can be an excuse for a caregiver to unleash injury.
    —in a letter from Mike Eigen,* March 13, 2008

not unordered in not resembling
    —Gertrude Stein, *Tender Buttons*

The possibility of envisioning bondage as a two-way affair, one side imprisoning crypt and the other a womb from which freedom is born, of seeing through to what dwells inside but otherwise outlives bondage . . .
    —Nathaniel Mackey, "Gassire's Lute"

Then there is the other, lonelier, powerless evocation of the will, which represents lingering desire without any hope or means of fulfillment, since all we have is the willing itself, supposed to be capable of magically turning thought into action, of unilaterally taking the place of all the now broken instruments of desire.
—MICHAEL WOOD, on Susan Sontag's *In America*,
Raritan, Summer 2001

A dream is real, a physical event, the body talking to itself.

When I read Keats's unfinished *Hyperion*s, I glimpse the remarkable drama of a poet "shamed by the knowledge that the gods are born once more of him, that great poetry must survive, if at all, in a cockney's breast."
—GEOFFREY HARTMAN, *A Scholar's Tale*

Humptydump Dublin squeaks through his norse;
Humptydump Dublin hath a horriple vorse.
But for all his kinks english plus his irismanx brogues
Humptydump Dublin's granddada of all rogues.
    —James Joyce, in *transition* 21

Our lives are worth more than their profits.
    —Olivier Besancenot, *The Nation*, June 16, 2008

... they still remembered tubercular or alcoholic beings who had died in the first years of the century, victims of rare words or punctuation.
    —Raymond Queneau, *The Last Days*

political correctness: what was left when socialism died.
    —Doris Lessing

A touching story of how a young fellow, protected alive by music and sex, outgrows his normal bedazzlement with Names and comes gradually to an inkling that there might be some real things and perhaps even other people.
    —Paul Goodman, a blurb for Ned Rorem's *Paris Diary*

 Tu réclamais le soir; il descend: le voici (Baudelaire, "Recueillement")
You cried for night; it falls: now cry in darkness (Beckett, *Endgame*)

The myth in a primitive society, i.e. in its original living form, is not a mere tale told but a reality lived. It is not in the nature of an invention such as we read in our novels today, but living reality, believed to have occurred in primordial times and to be influencing ever afterwards the world and the destinies of men.
—BRONISLAW MALINOWSKI, *Myth in Primitive Psychology*,
quoted by Charles Olson, the Olson/Creeley correspondence

That all things recur
is not the equal of the fact that they occur
—CHARLES OLSON, "The Post Virginal"

They do not hasten, each man hits in his place.
—WALT WHITMAN, "Song of Myself," 12

There was a Hungarian merchant who wanted, I don't know why, his son to learn Spanish. A student on holiday from Warsaw, who didn't know a word of that language, offered to give him lessons, and for several months diligently taught him Polish. If the boy had hoped, expected, thought or *known* that he knew Spanish, then when the truth came out, he would still have been free to accept that what he knew about his knowing Spanish was just to a very much greater degree not true than what he knew about other things about the world, and all the rest would depend on his sense of humour. Yet if he had *believed*, then he would have been bound not to let himself become convinced by the evidence, he would have had to think that the whole world was wrong and only he was right, he would have had to invent a faked universe all around him to suit his belief, and he would have had to come to the conclusion that the Polish translation of Cervantes was the original, and "Don Quijote de la Mancha," a Spanish translation from the Polish. And that is what believers do....
—STEFAN THEMERSON, *factor T*

. . . for rhythm was the wheel of Eternity, on which alone the transient and accidental could be broken, and the spirit set free.
 —Yeats, "Rosa Alchemica"

The substance if not the subject of film can only be the succession of present moments which it does not describe but *is*.
 —Geoffrey O'Brien, on Eric Rohmer, *NYRB*, October 23, 2008

Delocalization refers not only to the practice of moving production and services to where labor is cheapest, but also to the plan of destroying the status of all earlier fixed places so that the entire world becomes a Nowhere, and a single liquid market.
 —John Berger, *From A to X*

In his essay on Thoreau and Heidegger (!) [in *Philosophy the Day after Tomorrow*, Stanley] Cavell quotes Wittgenstein (whom he is always quoting, as if he can no longer tell his mind and Wittgenstein's apart): *Philosophy leaves everything as it is.* And then glosses it: "Wittgenstein may be seen as detecting and resisting philosophy's chronic tendency to violence, violence principally toward the ordinary, measured in its treatment of ordinary language, against letting it speak, having decided in time out of mind that it is vague and misleading, to say the least." I imagine William Carlos Williams reading this passage with joy.

. . . some late justification for the existence of collections and for places in which to exhibit their items in association with one another, as if the conditions of the makeup of the world and of the knowing of the world are there put on display and find reassurance.

Philosophers such as William James and John Dewey are forever appalled by what their fellow empiricists have been willing to settle for in the name

of experience, steadfastly refusing to give our birthright in return for, it may seem, so specialized a world, the world as required by the success of modern science.
 —STANLEY CAVELL, "The World as Things"

Asked once by a lady why he so constantly gave money to beggars, [Johnson] replied with great feeling, "Madam to enable them to beg *on*."
 —WALTER JACKSON BATE, *Samuel Johnson*

... a kaleidoscope endowed with awareness, which at each of its moments reproduces the multiplicity of life and the restless grace of all its elements.

Dandyism is a setting sun.
 —BAUDELAIRE, "The Painter of Modern Life"

December 15, '08, snowfall, big lazy flakes the size of Queen Anne's lace

You think me cold and do not see that I am imposing on myself an artificial calm.
 —BAUDELAIRE, in T. J. Clark, *The Image of the People*

There are gamblers equally fond of winning and losing.
 —BAUDELAIRE, *Years in Brussels*

Your attention will rest a little too long on the bluish clouds which are rising from your pipe. The idea of a slow, continuing, eternal evaporation will take hold of your mind and you will shortly apply this idea to your own thoughts, to your own brain. By a singular equivocation, by a kind of

intellectual transposition or misunderstanding you will feel as though you are evaporating and you will attribute to your pipe (inside which you feel yourself to be crouching, squashed up like tobacco) the strange power of smoking you.
    —BAUDELAIRE, *Poem of Hashish*

I like to imagine an art in which the quality of lastingness would be replaced by that of the provisional. An art constantly *applied* to life. Theaters. Seasons. Sunshine. Dancers and dancing.
    —BAUDELAIRE, *Years in Brussels*

For the final meaning of this play, whose glory it is to give itself so wholeheartedly to vulgarisation, I can only list a few approaches to its irony.... "this is always likely to happen; everything spiritual and valuable has a gross and revolting parody, very similar to it, with [the] same name; only unremitting effort can distinguish between them" (Swift) ...
    —EMPSON on *The Beggar's Opera*, in *Some Versions of Pastoral*

The *other words* to *The Waste Land*, Declaration of Independence, "Over the Rainbow," etc. That each work of art (literary) has another set of words to it. As in the oldtime obscene lyrics to straight popular tunes: "You came to me / And you were nowhere..."
    —BILL ZAVATSKY, notebook entry, in *Mulberry 3*

... the psyche, thinking or thoughtless, contains, if anything, layers of reality that wait. They are waiting for a style to surprise them, so that they may be spoken.
    —CHRISTOPHER MIDDLETON, "Introduction,"
      Lars Gustafsson, *The Stillness of the World before Bach*

A clearly defined object, independent and separate from all other objects and circumstances, in which we cannot see whatever we choose or make of it anything we want, whose meaning is not detachable or translatable. A free, unmanipulated and unmanipulatable, useless, unmarketable, irreducible, unphotographable, unreproducible, inexplicable icon. A non-entertainment, not for art commerce or mass-art publics, non-expressionist, not for oneself."

—AD REINHARDT, "The Black-Square Paintings"

At the book's climax, in a very curious phrase, when Moby Dick smashes the ship of his pursuers with "the solid white buttress of his forehead," he is seen "vibrating his predestinating head." Predestinating: the awful absence of God, of the Calvinist God, becomes, in a way, God. Moby Dick represents the utter blank horror of the universe if Godless, Melville has been described as a mystic, but to me he has nothing of mysticism such as might be ascribed to Wordsworth or D. H. Lawrence. Melville is a rational man who wants God to exist. He wants Him to exist for the same reasons we all do: to be our rescuer and appreciator, to act as a confidant in our moments of crisis and to give us reassurance that, over the horizon of our deaths, we will survive.

—JOHN UPDIKE, "Herman Melville's Soft Withdrawal,"
    The New Yorker, May 10, 1982

Kindness comes from what Freud called—in a different context—"after-education," that is, a revived awareness of something that is already felt and known. And this after-education ... entails the recognition of kindness as a continual temptation in everyday life that we resist. Not a temptation to sacrifice ourselves, but to include ourselves with others. Not a temptation to renounce or ignore the aggressive aspects of ourselves, but to see kindness as being in solidarity with human need, and with the very paradoxical sense of powerlessness and power that human need induces.

—ADAM PHILLIPS and BARBARA TAYLOR, *On Kindness*

I have always admired people who have left behind them an incomprehensible mess.
    —BOB DYLAN, in an interview

... suddenly, comes an insight, just a modicum, a microscopic "triumph" of order, in existence, as this or that set of words. Then the laughter is shaken out of the apple tree, as Tzara said: poetry becomes exploration beyond the frontiers of the ego.
    —CHRISTOPHER MIDDLETON, *The Pursuit of the Kingfisher*

I can think of few other artists so richly deserved by their times.
    —PETER SCHJELDAHL, on Martin Kippenberger,
        in *The New Yorker*, March 9, 2009

[Delmore] Schwartz's translation [of *A Season in Hell*] is considered to be sophomoric. Still, it might be sophomoric from the point of view of translating from one language into another and yet contain things that matter.

... it takes an unbelievable vigor to attach oneself to the things that smack one in the eye. It is so much easier to call a wheel a wheel than to see it as, say, Holbein would see it and to name its parts.
    —WALLACE STEVENS, *The Letters*

I would abhor a politics, pedagogy, or town-planning deduced from metaphysics or epistemology, or even scientifically deduced, rather than being pragmatic and not immoral. One must not manipulate real people because of an ideal or a confirmed hypothesis.

For me, the chief principle of anarchism is not freedom but autonomy, the ability to initiate a task and do it one's own way.... The aim of politics is to increase autonomy, and so it is mostly undoing. I like the Marxist formula "the withering away of the state," but it is the method, not the result.

The present, says Whitehead, is holy ground.
—Paul Goodman, *Little Prayers and Finite Experience*

... when the physician is diseased the disease comes to him as her lover to a virgin. He can't understand it.
—William Carlos Williams, letter to Kenneth Burke, November 1945

What you reveal in your letter over the Reich book is to me thrilling in the extreme, it seems to state or does state what seems to be the basic reason for our interest, our sustained interest in each other which has never been explicit—a desire on both our parts to find some basis for avoiding the tyranny of the symbolic without sacrificing fullness of imagery. ... My whole intent, in my life, has been as with you to find a basis (in poetry, in my case) for the actual.
—W.C.W., 1947 letter to K.B.

The steps in the poem seem to strike a series of glancing blows, as each moment of stability is found to contain an element of instability that requires you to hurry on.
—Kenneth Burke on W.C.W.'s "Song" ("beauty is a shell"), letter of June 25, 1960

My films are about timidity. My characters want to take part. They want to belong, and be like everybody else.
—François Truffaut, interview, quoted in Alan Bennett's diary entry for October 28, 1984

The map is not the territory.
—ALFRED KORZYBSKI, *Science and Sanity*

Rigor cleans the window through which intuition shines.
—ELLIS COOPER*

Children picking up our bones
Will never know that these were once
As quick as foxes on the hill
—WALLACE STEVENS, "A Postcard from the Volcano"

This unity finds expression in lack of differentiation between the word and the substance in the Hebrew tongue, and the relationship between the word and the substance is like that between *nefesh* and *guf* [the body]. In order to denote the absence of existence, non-being, the Hebrew says: as "naught" [*lo dabhar*, "no word"] = non-existent. For the existent finds expression only in action and movement, and if there is no action or movement, there is nothing [literally "no word"]. The *dabhar*, word, pertains only to that which exists; hence there is no difference between theory and practice, and there is no abstraction. Actuality is the fact of power and action, which are life. Life is conceived as power.
—EPHRAIM URBACH, *The Sages* (1975),
cited by Harold Bloom in *The Book of J*

Man, all of man, is a living soul, where the soul, *nefesh*, is not the *psyche* but all of a unified man. J's *nefesh* primarily means "life" yet just as well means "flesh." J's *ruah*, "breath" or "spirit," is the force that impels the *nefesh*, and thus is another manifestation of *nefesh* as life.
—HAROLD BLOOM, *The Book of J*

I have made scarcely any changes in the texts of the poems, since I'm fairly certain that, after a shortish time, the person through whom a poem was written is no more entitled to make revisions than any other reader.
 —Paul Muldoon, Author's Note to *Poems 1968–98*

"PSYCHOANALYSIS: THE MUSICAL"

Ashbery: his fluent exhaustion.

Thinking about the Jack Tworkov show: One of the premises of the New York School was that painters had insides. Warhol didn't think so.

We may live diminished lives in the midst of noise, of darkness, and of deadly exhalation. But the world cannot become a factory, nor a mine. . . . Neither the avarice nor the rage of men will ever feed them.
 —Ruskin, *Unto This Last*

All this disposal business, these basins, enamel buckets, plunging tubes, embalming sluices, constant jets, sterile bins, sealed incinerators, consideration of where the banjo-player might have gone that night, of the abolition of words taped to our memories, of the storage of one night under another night, the earlier ones gradually fading as the multi-track builds up beyond the bounds of desire; all this question of the attenuation of substance to concepts. . . .
 —Roy Fisher, *The Ship's Orchestra*

The more he looked
the more he saw
 —Roy Fisher, "The Six Deliberate Acts"

... How hard
is understanding? Some things
are lying in wait in the world,
walking about in the world,
happening when touched, as they must.
—Roy Fisher, "Staffordshire Red"

... romantics distrust engineers—sometimes correctly—for their hubris and are uncomfortable with the prospect of fixing things because the essence of tragedy is that it can't be fixed.
—Stewart Brand, *Whole Earth Discipline*

"In some languages," Austin observed, "a double negative yields an affirmative. In others, a double negative yields a more emphatic negative. It is curious, though, that in no language known to me, whether natural or artificial, does a double affirmative yield a negative." At which point Morgenbesser piped up from the back of the audience: "Yeah, yeah."
—Jim Holt, "Morgenbesserisms," *LRB* blog, September 22, 2009

a crumbling maze of an essay
—Benjamin Kunkel, on Javier Marías's *Negra espalda del tiempo*, *LRB* blog, December 3, 2009

But we must not call "duty," as we do every day, an inner bitterness and asperity that is born of private interest and passion; nor "courage," a treacherous and malicious conduct. Their propensity to malignity and violence they call zeal. It is not the cause that inflames them, it is their self-interest. They kindle war not because it is just, but because it is war.
—Montaigne, "Of the useful and the honorable"

Everything about his appearance proclaimed that he was less capable than anyone of launching himself upon the perilous path of personal example.
—ALFRED JARRY, *The Supermale*, trans. Barbara Wright

Fellini: the temptation of Saint Anthony.

Philosophy is a battle against the bewitchment of our intelligence by means of language.

A *picture* held us captive. And we could not get outside it, for it lay in our language and language seemed to repeat it to us inexorably.

What *we* do is to bring words back from their metaphysical to their everyday use.
—WITTGENSTEIN, *Philosophical Investigations*

The whole point about being at the races is that when you're there you're not in some dreary hospital, waiting to see how the surgery came out. Intelligent people understand that.
—DANIEL FUCHS, "Triplicate"

He was honorable, to be looked up to—a "delectable mountain," to use the phrase in the French novel by Alain-Fournier, *The Wanderer*.
—DANIEL FUCHS, "Strictly Movie"

but we wish the river had another shore,
some further range of delectable mountains,

distant hills powdered blue as a girl's eyelid.
—ROBERT LOWELL, "July in Washington"

Show at Asia Society, February 13, 2010

viet = people
nam = south
Viet Nam

Ganesha:
elephant-headed god
Lord of Obstacles
God of Wealth
first figure worshippers encounter at a Hindu temple
Shiva's son
sometimes holds a broken tusk, which he detached to use as a pen when he served as scribe for an Indian sage who was reciting the *Mahabharata*

Dharmapula: the eight guardians of the Law

Brahma: creator
Vishnu: preserver
Shiva: destroyer

Shiva:
linga (phallus)
Nataraja = Lord of the Dance, who dances the world into being and then destroys it

... bijou mash-ups of literary history

... the second-century fad for writing in the "Attic" dialect of democratic Athens (4th and 5th centuries BC), which used *tt* in place of the more regular *ss* (spelling the word for "sea" *thalatta* rather than *thalassa*, for example)

This preoccupation with classical diction—the origin of the modern Greek *katharevousa* or "pure" style

... the "Second Sophistic," a perilously vague term that scholars use, variously, to cover the era of Greek social history between 50 and 250 AD, the movement of literary classicism during that era, its preoccupation with rhetoric, and a supposed revival of Greek self-consciousness in the aftermath of absorption into the Roman Empire. Grecophone culture in the early empire was, however, extraordinarily diverse: how could a single formula (however hazily defined) capture such varied figures as the erotic novelist Achilles Tatius, the philosopher Sextus the Empiricist, the emperor Marcus Aurelius, the Christian apologist Clement of Alexandria, and Lucian? All of them were immensely erudite and rhetorically trained, and all worked within a tradition of classicising Hellenism; but in terms of social standing and literary output they could not be more different.
—Tim Whitmarsh, on Lucian, *LRB*, February 25, 2010

It assaults and pierces us to prayer when Odysseus descends into Hades to capture the flittering presence of his venerable mother: thrice he tries to take hold of her image: thrice she flies out of his hands. This is what the Greek Poets and Dante meant by transmigration, which is that reverend pilgrimage into other souls.
—Edward Dahlberg, *Can These Bones Live?*

. . . striking out toward the sublime in a vessel constructed of the commonplace, the neglected, the despised.
    —MICHAEL CHABON, *The Amazing Adventures of Kavalier & Clay*

Don't do anything that takes poems away from you!
    —CHRISTOPHER MIDDLETON

A poetry the quality of which
Is a stand made against intellectual apathy
    —HUGH MACDIARMID, "The Kind of Poetry I Want"

What is this imagining but the temptation to reckon that Blaff is a local operation of the large alternative to himself?

The multitude of infinitesimals, not the schema, is the source of good.

Well, you know what I mean, says Blaff with his shy insistence.

Will you plunge, as I never did, headfirst into the struggle, to give radiantly intelligent life away?

Beyond the scope of my messengers, resolute but dubious as they surely are, a place has yet to appear, a place that waits to house the urgent emptiness of me.

"The thing might be," he says, "to evolve a mode of knowing that actually takes up into itself the tangible, a subterfuge of domination and so becomes, not as now a little oilcan flourished in the face of the elements, but an all-sufficient element in itself, an agency that quells the rage of what in us corresponds to the elements, namely the distempered will."
    —CHRISTOPHER MIDDLETON, *Depictions of Blaff*

Meaning is a peculiar thing in poetry—as peculiar as meaning in politics or loving. In writing poetry a poet can hardly say that he knows what he means. In writing he is more intimately concerned with holding together a poem, and that is for him its meaning.
    —Edwin Denby, quoted in Bill Berkson, "Not an Exit"

Ezra, when a philosopher's speech is unsavory, indeed foul, of what use has philosophy been to him.
This needs no date—no question mark. It is for all time.
    —Marianne Moore, letter to Ezra Pound, early June 1955

old lunatic screech
asleep on the beach
face-down in the sand
must be the king of some heap
got his crown in his hand
well he'll tell us his story if he ever wakes up
but now he's bound for glory in a paper cup
    —Rachelle Garniez, "People Like You"

Pity is like rust to a cruel social machine.
    —Kurt Vonnegut, "In a Manner that Must Shame God Himself,"
        in *Wampeters*, etc.

... [Hesse's] holy wanderers ... resolve to keep out of taverns, though they miss the uncritical companionship they've had there.
    —Kurt Vonnegut, "Why They Read Hesse," in *Wampeters,* etc.

Not dispersed from one another, they move into a scheme that frees him and does without him.
    —Roy Fisher, "Metamorphoses"

"So what was it all about? [*Pull My Daisy*]"
"I think it was about the right to remain children."
  —Joyce Johnson, *Minor Characters*

Wang Wei is prized for his ability to turn language into miming gestures of the perceiving act.
  —Wai-Lim Yip, *Chinese Poetry*

Hans Hofmann: "In nature, light creates the sensation of color; in a picture, color creates light."

La simplicité même écrire
Pour aujourd'hui la main est là.★
  —Paul Éluard, "Confections"

I'm surrounded by mountains here
A circle of 108 beads, originally seeds
  of *ficus religiosa*
   Bo-Tree
A circle, continuous, one odd bead
Larger than the rest and bearing
A tassel (hair-tuft) (the man who sat
  under the tree)
In the center of the circle,
A void, an empty figure containing
All that's multiplied;
Each bead a repetition, a world
Of ignorance and sleep.
  —Philip Whalen, from "Sourdough Mountain Lookout"

de Kooning's women: Joan says they have his eyes, which are the one unmutilated feature, and which ask forgiveness.

de Kooning (as reported by Barry McCallion's father): "What does God care if I take a drink?"

. . . life's single lesson: that there is more accident to it than a man can ever admit to in a lifetime and stay sane.
—Thomas Pynchon, *V*

Ted Hughes, seeing the world's violence, makes it intentional, won't let go of volition. A world whose strife is that of the ego.

Irony is grief in a world where grief is impossible, a world without respite.

"Who is this person you are hurling through your own body?"

Les Six of one, half a dozen of the other.

This world is purgatory. I have plenty of proof that I am not damned—I understand that it is heretical to say so—but I am being tried, I have no notion why. Maybe that's what I'm supposed to learn.
—Paul Goodman, *Crazy Hope & Finite Experience*

The flowers Rousseau wanted for Apollinaire's portrait—*oeillets du poète*—are, in English, *sweet William*.

I have never known a foreigner less suited to Paris life.

The only person I have heard putting the case for cubism clearly and simply was Erik Satie.
>   —Fernande Olivier, *Picasso and His Friends*

Eros is fugitive, thus wingéd. Pornography would make it permanent. Which is death. Some art imitates life, some death.

The Cantos: that cork-lined room.

Language Poetry: it has no world.

Mother: stroke in April, heart attack in November. She died December 2, 1986.

"Myths pick *you*."

Blake [in *Jerusalem*]: The Last Judgment takes place in the loins.

I was the French professor. Like Laforgue.
>   —Marcel Duchamp, in Pierre Cabanne,
>   *Dialogues with Marcel Duchamp*

Beuys: warmth and self-determination as against materialist greed and alienation.

Nothing matters more, then, than that the people understand what is happening while it is happening.
—RONNIE DUGGER, *On Reagan*

Marsden Hartley's clotted, unattractive Dogtown Common paintings; and Philip Guston's late paintings; to turn against charm, finesse, winning. Athletes of refusal.

February 19, 1988: René Char died.

Bare night is best. Bare earth is best.
—WALLACE STEVENS, "Evening without Angels"

The drama of Char's syntax, the charged, overwrought verbal structures from which straight, brief declaratives emerge, like his lightning.

Elsewhere, work which emerges against a pressure to remain silent, some of its power the power of that struggle, lost in fluency.

"the body as capital"

Dream, July 26, 1980: I'm reading a book of aphorisms by Nietzsche: "Let him who has just carved a priest carve a crayfish."

It is only when many meanings are compressed into a single word, when depths of feeling are exhausted yet not expressed, when an unseen world hovers in the atmosphere of the poem, when the mean and common are used to express the elegant, when a poetic conception of rare beauty is

developed to the fullest extent in a style of surface simplicity—only then, when the conception is exalted to the highest degree and "the words are too few," will the poem, by expressing one's feelings in this way, have the power of moving Heaven and Earth within the brief confines of thirty-one syllables and be capable of softening the hearts of gods and demons.
> —the Priest Shun'e, replying to Kamo no Chōmei's
> question about what *yugen* meant

Ill the trees in gallows wood and they were innumerable in the forest of repression with its foliage so thick that, from dawn to dusk and from dusk to dawn one did not dare to imagine that some day, beyond the horizon and beyond habit, there would burst a scene all sulfur and love.
> —from a notebook of Arshile Gorky

Jewish tradition has it that each angel is created for a single purpose or mission, and that the angel has no choice but to fulfill its purpose, which is also its identity and its life-force. The instant an angel accomplishes its purpose, it ceases.
> —Allen Brafman

. . . the moon was a hieroglyph of exile
. . . citizens of a secret utopia
Heraclitus: the most powerful connections are the invisible ones.
. . . as a civilization I feel I am not really a part of moves into its third if not terminal millennium.
> —David Rattray, *How I Became One of the Invisible*

. . . obscenity of every description is one of the two great driving forces behind the ballet; the other is the belief in forgiveness and salvation.
> —Arlene Croce, *Going to the Dance*

The romantic movement with its turbulent heroism, its self-assertion, is over, superseded by a new naturalism that leaves man helpless before the contents of his own mind. One thinks of Joyce's *Anna Livia Plurabelle*, Pound's *Cantos*, works of an heroic sincerity, the man, his active faculties in suspense, one finger beating time to a bell sounding and echoing in the depths of his own mind.
    —YEATS, in his essay "Bishop Berkeley" (1931)

July 1995: Woke up one day thinking of a poem that you could go to day after day, that would be there, ready for whatever you might do.

Freud found Jung's statement "Sexuality destroys itself" a hopeless muddle. For Freud, the motif of self-sacrifice was a projection of repression, in which the conscious ego regretfully sacrificed its vigorous drives.

The problem of why the individual defends himself against sexuality can be approached on the basis of the fact that the sexual instinct is bipolar; it contains one component that calls for the dissolution of the ego.

... the idea that sadomasochistic phenomena represented an attempt to bind the degree of ego dissolution, to structuralize a universally present complication of sexual desire.
    —JOHN KERR, *A Most Dangerous Method*

I live to prevent someone from cracking up again.

To the Czech bourgeoisie Skvorecký gives wholly unironic praise: during its dark years under Communism, he suggests, it shed its worst qualities (smugness, philistinism, moral indifference), while these qualities passed, by the sleight-of-hand of history, to its persecutors. "How persistently they rose again ... not for the love of profit, but because they were the bourgeoisie, the underpinnings of the world. Diligent, capable, creative, stubborn, opinionated, incorrigible.... The only genuine creators of successful economic systems." (*Headed for the Blues*)

Olson's vision of Homer's *Odyssey* as a dance-drama in which a shaman-hero dances his way through a gauntlet of monsters to be reunited with a human other ...
    —Clayton Eshleman,
        "Seeds of Narrative in Paleolithic Art," *Sulfur* 23

The five desires: food, sex, sleep, fame, wealth.

January 1989: Jack Unterecker died
May 14, 1990: Mary Oppen died

That your note is part of a chord.

Not how the world is, is the mystical, but that it is.
    —Wittgenstein, *Tractatus*

A proverb is a ruin which stands on the site of an old story ...
    —Walter Benjamin, "The Storyteller"

The immobility of the Strayhorn ballad, and in much of Bill Evans: a music that does not move, that rocks in place, comes back to where it started. A kind of voluptuous inertia.

a man's *arete* = his potency as a fighter
oneirokrites = an interpreter of dreams

But the characteristic feature of shamanism is not the entry of an alien spirit into the shaman; it is the liberation of the shaman's spirit, which leaves his body and sets off on a mantic journey or "psychic excursion." Supernatural beings may assist him, but his own personality is the decisive element.

... the fragments of Empedocles are the one first-hand source from which we can still form some notion of what a Greek shaman was really like.

... but ritual is usually older than the myth by which people explain it.
—E. R. Dodds, *The Greeks and the Irrational*

.. the new Moloch, instantaneous information supplied readymade ...
—Christopher Middleton, *Crypto-topographia*

dialectical: "mutually determining"; "generative"
—notebook, New York, August 1982

Man's pride, which is fidelity to his limits, lucid love of his condition.
—Albert Camus, "Helen's Exile," in *The Myth of Sisyphus*

... myth (a word which among the Greeks meant nothing other than *the true word, the facts*, later *the facts about the gods*)
—Christa Wolf

Conversations with Frank Kuenstler

"I'm interested in Mallarmé as an extremist."
In Which: less like Virgil, more like David Jones
"The chickens of alienation have come home to roost."
"You start from a greater degree of deprivation."
"I know who my brother is."
"We live in an economy, but it's not a civilization."

February 7, 1996:
me: "What do you worry about?"
F.K.: "The inelasticity of the shoestring."

defending the "vanity" press: "those who wait for election when you could be creating value"

"There's a good argument for literature not having a life of its own."

Remember irony? Theory is what replaced irony.

. . . la chambre où je venais rompre avec toi le pain de nos désirs.★
    —Paul Éluard, "Nuits partagées"

the earth quaked
the milk shaked
the sun baked
the heart ached
    —Keely Garfield, *My Mother Was a Four-Alarm Fire*

Whitman: yielding, accepting, going with; the opposite of resistance, struggle

It is ourselves we organize in this way not against the past or for the future or even for survival but for integrity of understanding to insure persistence, to give the mind its stay.
—William Carlos Williams, *Autobiography*

Make it an invariable and obligatory law to yourself never to mention your own mental diseases.
—Johnson to Boswell in *The Life*

Fatalism, the sorrowful erasure of possibilities, is the philosophical problem at the heart of this book. To witness the intellectual exuberance and bravado with which the young Wallace attacks this problem, the ambition and elegance of the solution he works out so that possibility might be resurrected, is to mourn, once again, the possibilities that have been lost.
—Rebecca Newberger Goldstein, on David Foster Wallace's *Fate, Time, and Language: An Essay on Free Will*

Jim Rosen's work. One of his projects when I first knew him was the Sonoma County Camouflage Society. Painting can be revelation, an unveiling; Jim seems to go the opposite way, as if Salome put on veil after veil—Mallarmé's *pli selon pli*, but in reverse. Does this make me an incapable observer?

In other words, humans are unique as destroyers. There's never been anything like humans before on a global scale.
—E. O. Wilson

I began to notice a decade ago that the spirit of our time indulges in an inordinate amount of gratuitous meanness. Meanness: a withholding of generosity, a willingness to hurt, a perverse choice of the bad when the good is equally available.
—Guy Davenport, "A Letter to the Masterbuilder"

The day before yesterday this intertwined apple and pear were in full bloom. In every season these trees have been lovely, in autumn with their fruit, in winter a naked grace, in summer a round green puzzle of two kinds of leaves; but in spring they have always been a glory of white, something like what I expect an angel to look like when I see one. But I shall not see these trees again. Some developer has bought the property and cut down the embracing apple and pear, in full bloom, with a power saw, the whining growl of which is surely the language of devils at their business, which is to cancel creation.
—Guy Davenport, "Shaker Light"

Girlish, vivacious, and brash afternoon
That lifts with the wine of its wings
From the haunted seasons of yet to be
Summer's blond and Illyrian winters,
Launch the antique swan whose silence began
Under Babylon where the wisteria hung,
When he should have sung in the red pavilions
Passacaglia, toccata, and fugue,
The inward white of radiant space,
Cygnus and Betelgeuse and the Wanderers,
And swam instead but swan, exile and island and
Is now in this utter reality a brilliant ghost,
An archangelical, proud, fat bird,
Ignorant of what the stars intend by Swan.
—Mallarmé's "Le vierge, le vivace et le bel aujourd'hui,"
via Guy Davenport

Follow the breath
    —SALLY GROSS

[Robert Garioch] has an amusing story . . . about the time when, as a Scottish Episcopalian boy, he was due to be confirmed, and as part of the process had to confess which of the Seven Deadly Sins he was prone to commit. With humble but honest self-examination he goes through the list without finding anything, from Pride to Gluttony, that rings a bell. "The Rector grew impatient. 'You don't mean to tell me you're perfect?' he said. I said no, but whatever was wrong with me, it was not on the list."
    —EDWIN MORGAN

"All it takes," said Crake, "is the elimination of one generation. One generation of anything. Beetles, trees, microbes, scientists, speakers of French, whatever. Break the link in time between one generation and the next and it's game over forever."
    —MARGARET ATWOOD, *Oryx and Crake*

sing, refuse, transmute: to pose against give, sympathize, control

Sign over the urinal in the Grassroots Tavern, St. Mark's Place: DON'T BE FANCY, USE BOTH HANDS.

[Williams] takes from the *Wake* one sleeping giant, one hamadryad, and the radical idea that words go numb. And he also took, whether intentionally or not, the idea that where understanding fails the result is that we perceive a monster instead of an intelligible reality.
    —GUY DAVENPORT, "The House That Jack Built"

[*hamadryad*, from Greek *Hamadruas*, "one together with a tree," from *hama*, together with + *druas*, dryad, from *drus*, tree: A wood nymph living only as long as the tree of which she is the spirit and in which she lives. Brewer: Eurydice was a dryad.]

[Fairfield Porter's] art shares with the aesthetically more radical writing of Ashbery and Schuyler a cultivated sense of unhurried immersion in lived time, unfocussed but alert. Ashbery, a prolific creator, has said that writing poetry is like watching television: "There's always *something* on."
    —Peter Schjeldahl, "Artists and Writers,"
      The New Yorker, January 31, 2011

Pound: not history but a history of what is passing through his mind.

"Anti-semitism is the socialism of idiots.": in general use among German Social Democrats by the 1890s.

Go make today shine.
    —Andrew Bolotowsky,
        impromptu translation from an Italian aria

the junkyard of their power . . .
    —Salman Rushdie, *Luka and the Fire of Life*

I'm in love with eternity . . . I don't care about how many changes that go on, as long as it keeps going on.
    —Ornette Coleman, in Dick Fontaine's documentary
      David, Moffett, and Ornette

The only constant is a commitment to the thing that is song. This is in some way linked to the persistence of hope. Then as I get older this whole business of "song" only becomes still more mysterious. It is a plain bright mystery.
 —Denise Riley, in an interview on Shearsman Books blog,
  March 15, 2014

He was some kind of a man. What does it matter what you say about people?
 —Tanya (Marlene Dietrich) in *Touch of Evil*

He cherished magic because it put him in charge, so he never regarded it as a cheap trick.
 —David Thomson, on Orson Welles, *Rosebud*

And reassembling our afflicted Powers,
Consult how we may henceforth most offend
Our Enemy, our own loss how repair,
How overcome this dire Calamity,
What reinforcement we may gain from Hope,
If not what resolution from despare.
 —Milton, *Paradise Lost* I, 186ff.

Are the stairs those of the Hradˆcany, and are those holy figures meant who stand on the Karlsbrücke, something like a thirty-figure group? One should rather think of the 36 just men, who vouch their own lives to help the persecuted, who perhaps outweigh the extermination machinery of evil in the scales of time, to which in any case they don't leave the last word.
 —O. Pöggeler, on Paul Celan's "In Prag,"
  cited in Pierre Joris, *Breathturn*

I know no other grace than that of being born. An impartial mind finds this adequate.
—Isidore Ducasse (Lautrémont), *Maldoror*

                  Grace
to be born and live as variously as possible.
—Frank O'Hara, "In Memory of My Feelings"

Be reconciled, poet, with your world, it is
the only truth!
—William Carlos Williams, *Paterson* II

... the rest of life, the main thing ...
—Whitman, *Democratic Vistas*

"Artifact" is not even an adequate term to use in discussing the Maximus Poems: they are not the result of Olson's labors; they are his labors.
—Robert von Hallberg, *Charles Olson: The Scholar's Art*

These Days

whatever you have to say, leave
the roots on, let them
dangle

And the dirt

      Just to make clear
       where they come from
     —Charles Olson

The sane, Mr. Meagles intimates, are people plagued by suspicions of their own madness. Such life as they have is lived in quarantine. But people are always persecuted by what they protect themselves from.

. . . that, as a kind of word magic, if only we can get our definitions right, there will be no contagion. We will know where we are. But the will to conclusive definition is at best a sign of doubt, and at worst a sign of defeat.

an antithetical word; it keeps opposites in play

. . . to be ignored is one of the great freedoms.
 —Adam Phillips, *Going Sane*

We are children of chaos, and the deep structure of change is decay. At root, there is only corruption and the unstemmable tide of chaos. Gone is purpose; all that is left is direction. This is the bleakness we have to accept as we peer deeply and dispassionately into the heart of the universe.
 —Peter Atkins, *The Second Law*

Constance Repplier: "Be careful what you tell the unconscious."

John Wieners *is* her brother; they are brothers in a secret monastic order of poets who see everything as it is—fallen—at the same time as they remember a day when they didn't see it that way, when they saw it as all pulse and radiance and had a fine vocabulary to say so.
 —Fanny Howe, on Linda Norton,
  in her introduction to *The Public Gardens*

He is a metaphysician of the real, a metaphysician of flux and the things of this world, and has freed himself of systems of redemption.
 —from Armand Schwerner's statement on the back
  of Oppen's *Of Being Numerous*

Schwerner uses "metaphysician" as a condiment here; and I don't know if "[someone who] has freed himself of systems of redemption" can pass as a description of Oppen; it may describe me. "Freed himself" may be a little too august; gotten out from under, maybe. Walked away. Watched them recede.

. . . all is luminous in *Ark*; the spirit's resistance to splendor can be identified here—ominousness—but not examined.
    —Robert von Hallberg, on Ronald Johnson, in *Lyric Powers*

Just so: the spirit's resistance to splendor. Is it ungrateful to view splendor with suspicion? to want not to be overwhelmed?

Intermittent gods pass through our mortal amalgam without overstepping it. It is no limit to their adventure that we do not recognize them as divine.

To abolish distance kills. The gods die only from being among us.*

Obey your pigs, which exist. I submit to my gods, which do not.
    —René Char

I don't think it ever entered his mind that a poet could be critical of him.
    —Pierre Joris, on Heidegger, in *Justifying the Margins*

Every life viewed from the inside would be a series of defeats too humiliating and disgraceful to contemplate.
    —Orwell, on autobiography, in *Dickens, Dali & Others*

Progress is founded upon the experience of discordant feelings. Thus the contribution to Beauty which can be supplied by Discord—in itself

destructive and evil—is the positive feeling of a quick shift of aim from the tameness of outworn perfection to some other ideal with its freshness still upon it.
    —ALFRED NORTH WHITEHEAD, *Adventures of Ideas*

Christopher Middleton reading at Poets House. His voice is softer than I had imagined. He's having trouble with his eyes, so he read from pages that had been enlarged, interpolating remarks at will, full of lore. A likeable man! And a honeyhead. Completely unpretentious, tho decisive: when he was busy signing books afterwards he asked a friend to invite Yvonne Jacquette to join us for supper, but not the man she was talking to: "He is a bore." When someone tells him something that amuses him, or when he remembers something that does, he closes his eyes tight for a second or two, in some internal and private mirth, before opening them again to take you in and laugh aloud. At dinner he said he was reading Flann O'Brien, and when I told him that Dylan Thomas called *At Swim-Two-Birds* "just the sort of book to give your sister if she's a loud, dirty, boozy girl" he did that thing with his eyes.

When you run for your life part of it is likely to get caught in the door.

The art of the use of words would be a stain, a smutch, but for the stamina of things.
    —WALT WHITMAN, quoted in Robert von Hallberg,
        Charles Olson: The Scholar's Art

And another thing, you can't say *I love you* in Irish. Don't let them tell you otherwise. In Irish the love is on you. It's not yours to command.
    —DERMOT HEALY, *A Goat's Song*

> . . . complexity is not a crime, but carry
> it to the point of murkiness
>   and nothing is plain.
>   —Marianne Moore, "In the Days of Prismatic Color"

> everything resembles
> and everything is what it is
>   —Jerome Rothenberg, "Last Gnostic Hymn"

Lay on; bring to the fore; maximize. Instructions such as these seem to govern Manet's hand. By "maximize," I mean render the subject at its fullest, its most self-suffused. Let those cheeks be very, very bright, that riding habit wholly luscious in its blackness, that sky so very, very blue. Rendering whatever items commanded his attention, inducing them to exist on the canvas, was Manet's daily working agenda, whatever else may have passed through his mind. A robust, from-the-shoulder line of activity, like kneading bread or whisking cream, this way of his with dense and opaque colors: at the same time nimble, almost skittering, performed with a kind of exultation in its poise. And all the while, driven on by an anticipation of pleasure.
>   —Julian Bell

The way Monk questions a song. And the way it answers.

I could even bring some film of Frank and perhaps of Gail, if I can find it, and stuff we shot together one day of how people carry umbrellas. We had wild hopes of making a living recording unnoticed details of city life.
>   —letter from filmmaker Ken Jacobs,
>   on Frank and Gail Kuenstler

... his awareness of original sin, of the barrier that cuts off human beings from the enjoyment of the primitive Eden ...
—Gerald Brenan, on Góngora,
in *The Literature of the Spanish People*

The figure is nothing unless you twist it around like a strange miracle.
—Willem de Kooning

History does nothing, it possesses no immense wealth, it wages no battles. It is man, real living man, who does all that, who possesses and fights; "history" is not, as it were, a person apart, using man as a means to achieve its own aims, history is nothing but the activity of man pursuing his aims.
—Marx, *The Holy Family*

Labour as we know it is an alienated form of what [Marx] calls "praxis"—an ancient Greek word meaning the kind of free, self-realizing activity by which we transform the world. In ancient Greece, the word meant any activity of a free man, as opposed to a slave.
—Terry Eagleton, *Why Marx Was Right*

J'humilie maintenant à une pauvre fille au rire horrible ma bouche
—Apollinaire

(Beckett: "To a poor harlot horribly laughing I humble my mouth")

I wanted to eliminate all detail; all fact; and analysis; and myself; & yet not be frigid and rhetorical; & not monotonous (which I am) & to keep the swiftness of prose & yet strike one or two sparks, & not write poetical, but pure-bred prose, & keep the elements of character; & yet that there should be many characters and only one; & also an infinity, a background behind—well, I admit I was biting off too much.
—Virginia Woolf, on *The Waves*,
letter to John Lehmann, September 17, 1931

the dismal
fallacy that insistence
  is the measure of achievement
    —Marianne Moore, "In the Days of Prismatic Color"

... how life, from being made up of little separate incidents which one lived one by one, became curled and whole like a wave which bore one up with it and threw one down with it, there, with a dash on the beach.
—Virginia Woolf, *To the Lighthouse*

The disturbing thing about the whole process wasn't so much that the Tea Partiers were irrational as that they were irrationalist: they were consciously pursuing a course of action which made no economic sense, as part of a world-view which is essentially theological. They know that everyone else knows that they truly don't care about the consequence of their actions ...
—John Lanchester, *LRB*, September 8, 2011

Anybody ask you, baby, who was it sang this song,
Anybody ask you, baby, who was it sang this song,
Tell him little Jimmy Rushing, he's been here and gone.
    —"Baby Don't You Tell on Me"

A man, therefore, (so they say) should carry his profession or trade into prison with him if possible; if not, he must earn his living by the nearest thing to it that he can; but if he be a gentleman born and bred to no profession, he must pick oakum, or write art criticisms for a newspaper.

I know not why, but all the noblest arts hold in perfection but for a very little moment. They soon reach a height from which they begin to decline, and when they have begun to decline it is a pity that they cannot be knocked on the head; for an art is like a living organism—better dead than dying. There is no way of making an aged art young again; it must be born anew and grow up from infancy as a new thing, working out its own salvation from effort to effort in all fear and trembling.
    —SAMUEL BUTLER, *Erewhon*

By modernity I mean the ephemeral, the fugitive, the contingent, the half of art whose other half is the eternal and the immutable.
    —BAUDELAIRE, "The Painter of Modern Life"

… the slave-built gimcrack postmodernism of Dubai.
    —WILL SELF, *LRB*, October 20, 2011

An avenue wants to become a building.
    —LOUIS KAHN

In a review of a new biography of Ravel in the *LRB* [August 25, 2011], the reviewer [Stephen Walsh] tells a story recorded by Edward Lockspeiser in his life of Debussy:

... a remarkable conversation between Debussy and his old composition teacher, Ernest Guiraud, in which Guiraud plays a sequence of simple parallel chords and asks Debussy how he would "get out of this" (manage it, that is, as harmony that was going somewhere): "I'm not saying that what you do isn't beautiful, but it's theoretically absurd." "There is no theory," Debussy replies, "you have merely to listen. Pleasure is the law."

I asked the late great German novelist Heinrich Böll what the basic flaw was in the German character. He said, "Obedience."
—Kurt Vonnegut, *Timequake*

chickens:
white leghorns
bard rocks
ameriucanas
black austrolorps
cuckoo marans
red sexlinks

Up is higher than it seems.
—Sally Gross

... it would be of immense service to humanity if the Anglo-Saxon world could agree that all creative literature is Poetry; that prose is a form as well adapted for the utterance of poetry as verse.
—Ford Madox Hueffer [later Ford], *Thus to Revisit*

In his very sympathetic piece on Occupy Wall Street in *The Nation* Richard Kim speaks of "the common belief that capitalism is out of control and that the political system has broken down." But what if capitalism's nature and deepest desire is to *be* out of control, to refuse all regulation, even while professing to be self-governing? What if Norman Mailer got it right: "Capitalism . . . is essentially psychopathic. It lives for the moment. It can plan far ahead only at the expense of its own vitality."? And for whom has the political system broken down? Not for the people who own it, whom it services with zeal and efficiency. What is dawning on the rest of us is that there is no political system that represents us. Which is to say, things are even worse than we thought.

When I was publishing my *The Floor and the Breath* and Frank [Kuenstler]'s *In Which*, I said to Frank that I was worried about one of my poems. "What are you worried about?" he asked me. "I wish it was better," I said. "It's good enough," he said. Since then the notion of the poem that's good enough has seen me through many a bad patch.

"Is it very long?" Alice asked, for she had heard a good deal of poetry that day.
> —Through the Looking-Glass

. . . the lost language of a violent harmony
> —Michael Worton, on René Char, in his introduction to
> *The Dawn Breakers (Les Matinaux)*

"Socialism" is still the only word we have that attempts to bridge the gap between our private notions of decency and morality and the public sphere of the political economy. And it is still the only vision—the only modernist vision, that is—of a world in which individual desire might be reconciled with collective need. To neglect the socialist tradition as much

as Bellah and his colleagues do is to contribute to the impoverishment of the political imagination which they have so ably documented.
　—Barbara Ehrenreich, in George Scialabba,
　　The Modern Predicament

　the farthest thing away has one name, death,
and the other, the here and now, dumptruck.
　—Julio Cortázar, "Get a Move On," trans. Stephen Kessler

"I don't know how to stop," Coltrane complained to Miles Davis, who replied, "Take the horn out of your mouth."

The great actor and director John Cassavetes, discussing what he rated as a failed performance by a well-known actor in an acclaimed film he hated—Martin Sheen in *Apocalypse Now*—made a remark which haunts me in its implications: He said he thought Sheen might have been able to do something with the role, as badly written as he considered it to be, if as an actor he'd been allowed to insert some "stops" into the performance. What he meant by "stops," I believe, were simply gaps, or hesitations, actorly silences. Moments when thoughts left unexplored by the words themselves could be allowed to flood in. This possibility has always seemed to me a beautiful one, first for its craftsmanlike insight into the performer's art, but also in its suggestion that even a despised and oppressive text, a piece of junk like Cassavetes felt *Apocalypse Now* to be, might be worth this attempt at salvage. In other words, even a dishonest world might be worth trying to inhabit honestly.
　—Jonathan Lethem, *The Ecstasy of Influence*

Guston: art in sackcloth and ashes, penitent, forsaking an untenable sublime.

Since he never wrote anything long himself, perhaps he can be forgiven for never reading anything long either.
    —Colm Tóibín, on Borges

C.R., working on my neck, fired up the paresthesias in my legs in a sudden and painful way. I left very tired, thinking to go home and rest, but Joan had shopped, so there was food, which I cooked and we ate, and then I went to the film about Anselm Kiefer that I'd wanted to see. Waiting for it to start, I noticed great stiffness in my neck, and a headache centered on my right eye. That night I had a dream in which my body was rearranged (it was clearly my body, though I was seeing it from outside): my penis where my right eye had been, the eye where my penis had been. This sounds grotesque and frightful, but the dream was calm, as if to say, "This may take a little getting used to." I kept returning to it on Tuesday and Wednesday, turning over what it might mean. Wednesday morning, the word "cockeyed" presented itself to me, and I fell to thinking about Jean-Paul Sartre.

When I showed Frank my Éluard translations he said "I wish they were dirtier."

Art is hard enough without hanging "Life" on its shoulder, like some new kind of Original Sin.
    —Jonathan Williams

John Crawford's waitress-friend who once said to him "Crawf, you've got an Achilles heart."

Sweetest advice I ever got: when I told Stuart Miller that a translation of a Heine poem I hadn't looked at in a long while seemed more accurate than I had remembered, and lovely, he replied: "Faithful and lovely; so marry her."

I love art because it doesn't have rules like baseball. The only rule is to be good. That's the toughest thing to do.
    —Harry Callahan, via Jonathan Williams

The reciprocal civility of authors is one of the most risible scenes in the farce of life.
    —Samuel Johnson, *The Life of Sir Thomas Browne*

No beginnings, no endings.
    —Sally Gross

. . . capitalism, which is indifferent to group or individual survival . . .
    —Gideon Lewis-Kraus, on Peter Corning's
    The Fair Society, *LRB*, February 9, 2012

Circumcision of a heart
driven outside its secret
Elysian solitary imagination
by doubt but not by sight
    —Susan Howe, "Silence Wager Stories,"
    The Nonconformist's Memorial

The poem is the blind man's cane.

MY QUAKER-ATHEIST FRIEND, WHO HAS COME TO THIS MEETING HOUSE SINCE 1913, SMOKES & LOOKS OUT OVER THE RAWTHEY RIVER TO HOLME FELL

what do you do
anything for?

you do it
for what the medievals would call
something like
the *Glory of God*

doing it for money,
that doesn't do it;

doing it for vanity,
that doesn't do it;

doing it to justify a disorderly life,
that doesn't do it

look at Briggflatts here . . .

it represents the best
that the people were able to do

they didn't do it for gain;
in fact, they must have
taken a loss

whether it is a stone next to a stone
or a word next to a word,
it is the *glory*—
the simple craft of it

and money, and sex aren't worth
bugger-all, not
bugger-all

solid, common, *vulgar* words

the ones you can touch,
the ones that yield

and a respect for the music . . .

what else can you tell 'em?
    —Jonathan Williams

Now Big Oil's servants in Congress want to prevent any environmental review of the Keystone XL pipeline project, to insist on its passage without such a review. This seems to go past the irresponsible into the insane. Their bedrock conviction is that any environment exists only to be exploited, and that any regulation is an intolerable infringement on their liberty. Enormous determination not to know the consequences of their acts, or not to believe those consequences will come to pass, or that they will come to pass, but not for them. For the others. Or to know all of it and not care. When they've made their world unlivable. Is this not death wish? What their appetite is finally for?

Don't talk to capitalism about its principles. Capitalism has no principles, it's a desperate, ecstatic improvisation.

Poetry differs from prose because it only refers to itself; it can only be explained in its own context, on its own terms.
  —Eugenio Montale

. . . The real

is always worth the act of
lifting it, treading it

to be clear, to make it

clear (to clothe honor
anew
  —Charles Olson, *The Maximus Poems*, "Letter 20"

... all

is how the splendor is worn. . . .
    —Olson, "Maximus, at Tyre and at Boston"

Numbers will do anything for you. Anything.

Suddenly, when he least expected it, the destiny of his family had put out a tendril to involve, to envelop him, and had drawn him back to itself and planted him there, grafting him, re-attaching him to the root from which he had been torn; making him feel all that he had always refused to feel, remember all that he had always refused to remember.
    —Luigi Pirandello, *The Old and the Young*

Persephone est, et Plutus senex, aurum hic, flos illa.

What allegiance, what bright recognition these poems moved in him . . . [Stesikhoros, Simonides]

I need to be near processes which are not destructive, no matter what else they might be.

The real world is what is left unsaid when we have said everything. What we have said is language and the world is not language. A rock is not a word.
    —Guy Davenport, "The Dawn in Erewhon"

a smile masturbates softly in the vacant
lot of his physiognomy
    —E. E. Cummings, of a politician, in *Is 5*

With this system, I'll soon make a fortune: then I'll kill everyone in the world, and go away.
—KING UBU, Jarry, *Ubu Roi*

Aldebaran. A double star in the constellation Taurus, one of the brightest stars in the sky. [from Arabic *al-dabarān*, "the follower (of the Pleiades)": *al*, the + *dabarān*, following, from *dabar*, to follow.]

W. G. Sebald called László Krasznahorkai's *The Melancholy of Resistance* "a book about a world into which the Leviathan has returned."

<u>Vonnegut's list</u>
Roberts Rules of Order
the Bill of Rights
the 12 Steps (A.A.)
Lincoln's Second Inaugural
the Sermon on the Mount (Matthew 5–7)
    —in *Slapstick* (and elsewhere)

George [Antheil]'s tastes and mine, as far as *Ulysses* was concerned, were similar. It "works," said George. He spoke of it as though it were a mechanical invention.
—SYLVIA BEACH, *Shakespeare and Company*

Interviewer: There is one more death in the background: the one of cinema. You are one of the few who still hold on to 35 mm film.
Aki Kaurismäki: Real film is light; digital is electricity.

Most of the emotions triggered by the best jazz are abstract: the hair stands up on your neck, and you shiver a little. But Davis, fed by Evans, is

telling you, in his monosyllabic way and with his long, vibratoless notes, about his life, about how sad it has been, about how he pities himself. He is not telling you how hard it is to be black; he is telling you how hard it is to be Davis. . . .
 —WHITNEY BALLIETT, *Collected Works: A Journal of Jazz*

You are comfortable enough a friend to have noticed by this time that I get along with people who don't expect a great deal and regard life as an existence to be got through with patience rather than a party to be enjoyed.
 —GUY DAVENPORT, letter to Jonathan Williams,
  in *A Garden Carried in a Pocket*

dilemma, 2. *Logic.* An argument in which a choice of two or more alternatives, each being conclusive and fatal, is presented to an antagonist. (*American Heritage Dictionary*)

Nietzsche (according to D. S. Carne-Ross): art the augury of restored wholeness

Kenneth Cox: his work as a cryptographer during the war was the best possible preparation for a life of writing lucidly about modernist poetry. I remember, and a lot of people remember, the vertiginous horror with which one stumbled across the Cantos for the first time; but Cox's work during the war was based on a faith in intelligibility, that what he was working on was meant to conceal the intelligible, one only had to tease it out. If you believe it's there, you're halfway home.

Don't bother to learn how to die. When the time comes for you to die you will know how to do it well enough.*
 —MONTAIGNE, "Of Physiognomy" (paraphrased by Harold Bloom)

Caledonian antisyzygy: Originally a learned joke of Gregory Smith's (he thought it might have amused both Sir Thomas Urquhart and Sir Thomas Browne) Smith defined it as "the sudden jostling of contraries" characteristic of Scottish literature. Recently George Elder Davie (in *The Crisis of the Democratic Intellect*, Edinburgh, 1986, 115) rendered the word as "unyokeableness." The French language has a similar expression: *une douche écossaise*, hot and cold alternating unmixed, likewise praise and reproof etc. But Buthlay understands "antisyzygy" to include any relation whatever between pairs of contraries. A dualistic welter drowns the specific sense of jostling, unyokeable, unaccomodating nextness. To insist on that sense is not to deny the lability of MacDiarmid's concepts. On the contrary it is to protect it. It is by means of words not themselves labile in meaning that the lability of concepts succeeds in being conveyed.
—Kenneth Cox, "Hugh MacDiarmid," *The Art of Language*

Nor is there any evidence that the slightest beam of moral insight into his own villainy ever penetrated Himmler's awareness. He was like those malefactors in Dante's hell who must remain there forever, precisely because they are completely unable to understand why they are there.
—Christopher Clark, *LRB*, October 11, 2012

To Jarry in 1898 [clinamen] signified the very principle of creation, of reality as an exception rather than the rule.
—Roger Shattuck, introduction to *Selected Works of Alfred Jarry*

Mistrust of life: Pascal.

A book is closed. You have to open it to read it.
—Colm Tóibín, interview on NPR, November 13, 2012

[Castiglione] extols *sprezzatura*: the art of doing everything gracefully and well, without the appearance of effort.
 —Hilary Mantel, *Wolf Hall*

I say these things to indicate in shorthand that I am not lost in Liberal psychology and do not consider Freud, Marx, and Spock a norm of sanity. Clarity, energy, outwardness, selflessness, lovingkindness—who will build a psychology on *them*?
 —Guy Davenport, letter to Jonathan Williams,
  in *A Garden Carried in a Pocket*

The author is made bigger by the range and sublimity of his model.
 —Darin Strauss, on Michael Chabon's
  Telegraph Avenue, *Ulysses* behind it,
  The New York Times, December 7, 2012

Debussy remarked that this air [Rameau's "Nature, amour"] was so individual and modern that one should be able to go up to Rameau after the performance and congratulate him.

. . . the great chaconnes that end each opera, the classic form of cyclical harmony and order restored . . .
 —Robert Mealy

[Siegfried Kracauer's] *American Writings* includes the endearing "Talk with Teddie," Kracauer's notes following a 1960 visit with Theodor Adorno and his wife Gretel. According to Friedel (as Kracauer's German friends called him), he jousted with Adorno over the logic of "Utopian thought" and, invoking Benjamin, told his friend that his vaunted dialectic was like a film consisting "exclusively of close-ups."

... "You cannot upset Teddie," Kracauer writes. "He grabs everything he is told, digests it and its consequences and then takes over in a spirit of superiority." Still, he concludes, "in spite of its emptiness, Teddie's output appears to be concrete and substantial. This semblance of fullness probably results from his aesthetic sensitivity."
—J. HOBERMAN, on Kracauer, *The Nation*, December 19, 2012

The titles *Public Safety, Montagnards, Girondins, Jacobins* and so on cannot be used in this republican Socialist movement. What we represent is the period which has passed between '93 and '71, with the genius which should characterize us and spring from our own temperament. This seems to me the more obvious in that we are like plagiaries, re-establishing to our own detriment a Terror that is not of our time. Let us employ the words suggested by our own revolution.
—GUSTAVE COURBET

Robert Archambeau, writing about Peter O'Leary's "Apocalypticism": "the essay argued that apocalypse—a sacred expression that can 'unbind love from material desire, freeing it to embrace the unknown and the unspeakable'—has been erased from American poetry."

What's wrong with material desire?

Every nuance takes you farther.
—SALLY GROSS

I asked Jack, who's had open heart surgery, how he was doing: "I'm somewhere between lethargy and terror."★

Avalokiteśvara: "[He who] hears the sounds of the world."

The cat, with eyne of burning coal,
Now couches fore the mouse's hole
    —*Pericles*, Chorus III, 5–6

Bawd: ... for your bride goes to that with shame which is her way to go with warrant.
Boult: Faith, some do, and some do not....
    —*Pericles,* IV, ii, 119f.

Il y a assurément un autre monde mais il est dans celui-ci.★
    —PAUL ÉLUARD

the laughter of unease
    —FREUD

Objection, evasion, joyous distrust, and love of irony are signs of health; everything absolute belongs to pathology.
    —NIETZSCHE, *Beyond Good and Evil*

... the mystifications and banalities that spread like stains, or bad prose, from the people in power.
    —CHRISTOPHER MIDDLETON

Certainly the writer today has to be on guard against totalitarian urges and influences, in so far as he feels them to be deadly falsifications of human reality. He has to distinguish very sharply between true and false conceptions of totality. His best energies may be articulated in archipelagos of fragments (René Char).

Is any true totality even faintly conceivable to us? If not, then how can we concretely and actually identify what is meant by the cliché "false totality"?

In our bones we know what it means. We can see it every day in the bulging trouser-bottoms of American executives; we see it in the scowls on the faces of Greek plainclothes policemen; we see it in the hecatombs of children, the economically motivated massive destruction of human lives in Vietnam; we see it in the slaughter of Indian populations in Brazil, and in the torturing of political dissidents there and elsewhere. I doubt if we go wrong if we call it terror, which is dead magic. But to so many people it brings a sense of ease, because a reality is provided, because you do not have to create a reality out of questions and spontaneous desires. What about true totality? It is an aspect of what Paul Celan called "the majesty of the absurd," that some writers can still live and swear by the living magic of suggestion, as the only open gateway to true totality in linguistic structures. A few fine details, but they point a way into the interior, from which flows a light that is inextinguishable. Who is ever admitted? Nobody is in there all the time.

—CHRISTOPHER MIDDLETON, *Bolshevism in Art*

Let the winds of dawn that blow
Softly round your dreaming head
Such a day of sweetness show
Eye and knocking heart may bless,
Find the mortal world enough

—W. H. AUDEN, "Lay your sleeping head, my love,"

Charges that someone is a fraud or charlatan amount usually to a base and envious reaction by those who distrust a species of mental power: ironic, agnostic, riddling, skeptical.

—GEOFFREY HARTMAN, *A Scholar's Tale*

If you put the sun inside your trousers, all you do is burn your trousers and wet the sun. This is what happened to [Musset]. Nerves, magnetism: for him poetry is those things. Actually, it is something less turbulent. If sensitive nerves were the only requirement of a poet, I should be superior to Shakespeare and to Homer, whom I picture as a not very nervous individual.
 —Flaubert, *Letters to Louise Colet*

Without love's eyes art sees no sensible life.
 —Louis Zukofsky, *Bottom: On Shakespeare*

This is a world poetry alone experiences. Its practise is its theory and texts beg no improvement from "ingenious" editors.
 —Cid Corman, on Zukofsky's Shakespeare

Charlie Parker was a genius, and the young Louis Armstrong was too. Their music burst out of them as flashes of insight. It seemed to depend more on intuition than on introspection, and once they were rightly heard all the music around them had to change.
 —Jack Chambers, *Milestones: The Music and Times of Miles Davis*

John Coltrane . . . whose final torrential performances might be heard as a compulsive search for a way out of a self-generated impasse.
 —Geoff Dyer, "In Transit," *LRB*, June 20, 2013

One night [Monk] asked Motian to sing him his cymbal beat. He did, and Monk thought about it and sang a corrected version back to him, with a tiny bit more emphasis on the last stroke of the triplet.
 —Ben Ratliff, *The Jazz Ear*

Get over it. There are things we don't get over because they have made us what we are. And how do you get over what you are?

Meanwhile I saw Jarrell; I gave a lecture in North Carolina and he introduced me. Now he is off to a mental hospital, Cal told me. He seemed quite sick when I saw him, chiefly depressed but with some streak of real insanity in it that frightened me; as though some altogether alien person was looking through him who still was He.
—Hannah Arendt, in a letter to Mary McCarthy, April 1965

In 1983 Caravan of Dreams, an arts center, opened in Fort Worth. Its director was Kathelin Hoffman. Ornette Coleman's "Kathelin"?

Boulez assumes, not historically but personally, that Debussy's problem lay in how to "deal with" tonality. *Mais non, Madame, la peinture est plus bête que cela*, retorted Degas to a dilettante ingratiator blasting her pale fire. All great art is dumb, inviolable to the theorizing madmen banging their heads against—strewing their brains upon—the pristine marble.
—Ned Rorem, *Setting the Tone*

Just when the gods had ceased to be, and the Christ had not yet come, there was a unique moment in history, between Cicero and Marcus Aurelius, when man stood alone.
—Flaubert, letter to Madame Roger des Genettes

Those who know nothing, love nothing; those who do nothing, understand nothing.
—quoted in Guy Davenport, "The Scholar as Critic,"
in *Every Force Evolves a Form*

Nihil in intellectu quod prius non fuerit in sensu.*—Aquinas, after Aristotle
Say it, no ideas but in things—WCW

I don't care who I am. I don't care who you are. I care about the current we conduct.
    —Michael Hamburger

The call upon history will seem uncongenial with Wittgenstein. He seems so ahistorical. —He is ahistorical the way Nietzsche is atheistical. (Call these desires for awakening.) And aphilosophical in this way. Because what can come between us is, also, philosophy. There may be ultimate philosophical differences. But if there are they should not be caused by philosophy itself.

To let yourself matter is to acknowledge not merely how it is with you, and hence to acknowledge that you want the other to care, at least to care to know. It is equally to acknowledge that your expressions in fact express you, that they are yours, that you are in them. This means allowing yourself to be comprehended, something you can always deny. Not to deny it is, I would like to say, to acknowledge your body, and the body of your expressions, to be yours, you on earth, all there will ever *be* of you.
    —Stanley Cavell, *The Claim of Reason*

To suggest that his thinking was aberrant is to deny the magnitude of the problem he presents.
    —Lucy Hughes-Hallet, *Gabriele D'Annunzio*

Every great artist, at his beginning, remakes the whole art to his own image.
    —Victor Hugo, quoted by Simon Leys,
        "Victor Hugo," in *The Hall of Uselessness*

It is not all poetry that is betrayed when it is given the voice of philosophizing discourse: only that poetry whose difference is taken away when philosophy speaks it.
 —J. M. COETZEE, *Giving Offense*

hafiz, a Moslem who has memorized the Koran, from Arabic *hafiza*, watch, protect, memorize

Democracy is like blowing your nose—you may not do it very well, but you ought to do it yourself.★
 —GARRY WILLS, *Outside Looking In*,
  citing, but starkly paraphrasing, G. K. Chesterton

His concern to produce an individual structure of perception for every place, thought and experience he writes about results in a ceaseless and challenging originality.
 —ALAN BROWNJOHN, on Christopher Middleton,
  in the *New Statesman*

always curious about the body
 —SALLY GROSS

Le poème est ascension furieuse; la poésie, le jeu des berges arides.★
 —RENÉ CHAR, *Feuillets d'Hypnos*

To an interviewer who asked if he did not regret having spent more time reading than living, Borges replied, "There are many ways of living, and reading is one of them."

Bread & Puppet Theater: "At the moment when the first atomic bomb was dropped, Oppenheimer, the chief architect of that bomb, recalled words from the Bhagavad Gita, the Hindu prayer book: 'Life, the splendor of 1000 suns blazing all at once, resembling the exulted soul, is become Death, the shatterer of worlds.' The overt extrajudicial capabilities of the society system allow the shatterer of worlds to function legally to cultivate destructions so minute and gigantic, the eye cannot perceive and the mind cannot behold them. No politician, no hazardous substance, but a well-established tradition and demon strengthened by endless practices of devastation, the shatterer continues to plot the assassination of existence-as-it-is, while disguising his activities as benevolent maneuvers meant to cure the two ailing adversaries: the planet and humanity. By imitating the miraculous blossoming of the evening primrose, the Shatterer of Worlds Chapel manages to reverse the original statement: Death, the shatterer of worlds, becomes Life, the splendor of 1000 suns blazing all at once, resembling the exulted soul."

the Department of Convenient Emotions

Again the three ethnographers pay close attention: they are members of a generation of gringos who worry about the way their society seems bent on the destruction of the earth, the biosphere itself.
    —Dennis Tedlock, *Breath on the Mirror*

Allen Brafman on the Ray Charles stamp: "smiling the grandfather of all smiles, smiling as though he has invented joy."

. . . David Smith's openness—he was never on guard, except that he would not say anything against a fellow artist, because by having that life commitment, he was beyond reproach . . .
    —Robert Motherwell, "A Recollection of David Smith
       and the 1950s," in *Writings*

And it's all the more moving, to me, because the stance is so devoid of fanaticism—is, rather, generous & open to . . . other poets, rejecting few in his own thought, whatever crankiness he may show as a matter of style or instance. ("How can I reject *anyone* who's risked this much?" he said to me with respect to my own work with anthologies & the need to exclude therefrom, etc.) An inclusive rather than an exclusive avant-garde, then . . .
    —Jerome Rothenberg on Jackson Mac Low,
       in *Poetics and Polemics*

Le poète est maçon, il ajuste des pierres, le prosateur cimentier, il coule du béton.*
    —Pierre Reverdy, *Le Livre de mon bord*

The failure on our part to accept the reality of pain, of anguish, of ambiguity, of death, has turned us into a very peculiar and monstrous people. It means, for one thing, and it's very serious, that people who have had no experience have no compassion.
    —James Baldwin, "The Uses of the Blues"

absolute originality, the intensive, often grotesque expression of force and life in the simplest form
    —Emil Nolde, diary entry concerning tribal art in the Pacific

Birds fly because they have more imagination.
    —Darrell Gray, via Merrill Gilfillan

In the asylum, asked if he was writing anything, Robert Walser replied, "I am not here to write, but to be mad."

For the right names of flowers are yet in heaven.
  —Christopher Smart, *Jubilate Agno*

The marks of the Buddhist teachings are impermanence, no-self, the inevitability of suffering, interconnectedness, emptiness, the vastness of mind, and the provision of a Way to realization.
  —Gary Snyder, introduction to *Beneath a Single Moon*

Adam Mars-Jones on *Not I*: "Beckett had a clear idea of the effect he wanted to produce with the monologue, an orifice vomiting language ('an organ of emission, without intellect') . . ."

Lawrence's jeering: he was determined not to be depressed.

Oh he closes his eyes when he kicks you,
For a cat cannot look at a queen . . .
  —Rachelle Garniez

Jarry: "his violated life"
  —Roger Shattuck

Consider well the proportions of things. It is better to be a young June bug than an old bird of paradise.
  —*Pudd'nhead Wilson's Calendar*

It turned out our grip on these things [nuclear weapons] was tighter and our attraction to them was deeper or stranger than the reasons we gave ourselves during the forty-plus years of the Cold War.
 —Jonathan Schell, in conversation with Bill McKibben,
  The New Yorker, April 7, 2014

Remembering the reading series at the Guggenheim in the '60s: the microphone was attached to a cord which was placed around the reader's neck, so each poet was ceremoniously hanged before proceeding.

Sexual frenzy was as respectable a passion to Sappho as rapacious selfishness to an American.
 —Guy Davenport, introduction to *Archilochos, Sappho, Alkman*

"Beauty Riding an Ox beneath a Willow" (scroll by Utagawa Toyoharu)

The breath is the practice.
 —Sally Gross

Poets and beggars, musicians and prophets, warriors and scoundrels, all creatures of that unbridled reality, we have had to ask but little of imagination. For our crucial problem has been a lack of conventional means to render our lives believable.
 —Gabriel García Márquez,
  "The Solitude of Latin America: Nobel Prize Address, 1982"

Paint, not the thing, but the effect it produces.
 —Mallarmé, letter to Henri Cazalis, October 1864

In serene souls there is no wit. Wit testifies of a disturbed equilibrium; it is the result of the disturbance and, at the same time, the means of restoring the equilibrium. Passion commands the most violent form of wit. The state in which all our relationships break up, that of despair or that of spiritual death, is the most terrifyingly witty of all.
—NOVALIS, "Pollen"

One is an artist by virtue of experiencing what non-artists call "form" as content.
—NIETZSCHE, *The Will to Power*

Sergius lay his hands on the table. His plane by now gone. This, all this, as it was meant to be. Sergius, arrived here in this crucial indefinite place, this undisclosed location, severed from the life of the planet yet not aloft. Arrived at last at this nowhere in which he became visible before the law.
A cell of one, beating like a heart.
—JONATHAN LETHEM, the end of *Dissident Gardens*

The wealthiest of the wealthy now view art as an alternative currency.
—*The New York Times*, July 8, 2014

It seems to me that all social scientists, all journalists and commentators, all activists in the unions and in politics of whatever stripe, and especially all citizens should take a serious interest in money, its measurement, the facts surrounding it, and its history. Those who have a lot of it never fail to defend their interests. Refusing to deal with numbers rarely serves the interests of the less well-off.
—THOMAS PIKETTY, *Capital in the 21st Century*

Better awkward than clever, better ugly than charming, better fragmented than slick, better straightforward than calculating.
—Fu Shan (1607–1684) on calligraphy

Death enters into everything we undertake, and it is no longer a transition but a great gaping mouth that nothing can satisfy.
—Octavio Paz, *The Labyrinth of Solitude*

Olson: History is the story of his finding out, not what he finds.

What is more comic and terrible than the angular intellectual proud woman approaching God inch by inch with ground teeth?
—Flannery O'Connor, 1955 letter to "A",
discussing Simone Weil, in *The Habit of Being*

On a beam supporting the ceiling of Brecht's study are painted the words "Truth is concrete." On a window sill stands a little wooden donkey that can nod its head. Brecht has hung a little notice around its neck saying "I, too, must understand it."
—Walter Benjamin, diary entry, July 24, 1934, *Reflections*

Did anyone think that craft was mastery? It is hardly anything but loss, even with the enormous gain of word upon word sent, surging, staggering into a void that the poet is as eager to enter as the spirit of Arnaut Daniel was to leap back into the refining fire.

What coral gestures should I make to ward off the nixies lurking round this moxie?
—Rachel Blau DuPlessis,
Blue Studios: Poetry and its Cultural Work

I owe CM a debt of understanding. At a time when the Sunday broadsheets still carried reviews of new poetry there appeared a review of his book *Torse #3*. The piece was by its own standards civilized: but it was patronizing, ignorant, insular and weary. I had at that time virtually no contacts and no prospect of getting a book published; but I was working tentatively in a distant corner of the same territory, and the review showed me in an instant how the cards were stacked. It freed me from setting any store by opinions that might come from such a quarter.
 —Roy Fisher, *Tributes to Christopher Middleton*,
  The Bow Wow Shop (online blog)

Artists find their own way and no other way makes sense to them.
 —Joan Farber

The greatest threat to a pure artist is the power that society has to assimilate him and make him into one of its ornaments.
 —Wallace Fowlie, on Genet, *Journal of Rehearsals*

Her art examines the aesthetics of that strange half-life when things, people and the stories they tell have become obsolete but insist on hanging around.
 —Brian Dillon, on filmmaker Tacita Dean

The sound of the band was almost a reduction to an inactivity of music, to a stillness. Everything—melody, harmony, rhythm—was moving at minimum speed. The melody was very slow, static; the rhythm was nothing much faster than quarter notes and a minimum of syncopation. Everything was lowered to create a sound, and nothing was to be used to distract from that sound. The sound hung like a cloud.
 —Gil Evans, describing the Claude Thornhill band,
  in a 1957 *Downbeat* article

The source of a phrase my mother loved: In 1886 President Grover Cleveland sent a message to Congress that touched on the disuse into which the once-controversial Tenure of Office Act had fallen: "After an existence of nearly 20 years of almost innocuous desuetude, these laws are brought forth."

The pure intervals of the overtone series do not provide a practical basis for tuning keyboard instruments unless there are something like 32 keys per octave instead of the 12 we commonly have. The pure intervals are compromised to form bearable approximations of true resonance. But strings resonate as nature intended them, with pure overtones, close enough to the compromised frequencies to cause the tuned strings to vibrate sympathetically with them. The result is a magnificent haze.
  —Nancy Garniez,* program note for "Mixed Bag"
      recital, October 2014

Nancy Garniez told me this story: The cadence of the slow movement of Ursula Mamlock's *Wind Quintet*, intricately voiced counterpoint that ended on a minor triad. Milton Babbitt told her, "If you write cadences like that you'll never have a career!"

The Moods

Time drops in decay,
Like a candle burnt out,
And the mountains and woods
Have their day, have their day;
What one in the rout
Of the fire-born moods
Has fallen away?
        —Yeats

My unique relation—and it a tenuous one—is the making relation. I am with it a little in the dark and fumbling of making, as long as that lasts, then no more. I have no light to throw on it myself and it seems a stranger in the light that others throw.
—Beckett, letter to Arland Ussher, 1962

Did you know her.
Did you love her, brother.
Did wonder pour down
on the whole goddamn town.
—Robert Creeley, "The Memo"

... the terrible babble of things, the very *undertone* of consumer society, our colonized unconscious
—Olivier Assayas

White thy fambles, red thy gan
And thy quarrons dainty is.
Couch a hogshead with me then.
In the darkmans clip and kiss.
—*Ulysses*, "Proteus"

blue simple horizon of all care
World as it is when I am not there.
—Anne Carson, "Decreation Aria"

Growing up in Ireland, we didn't need aliens—we already had a race of higher beings to gaze deep into our eyes and force us to have babies against our will: we called them priests.
—Anne Enright, *Making Babies*

Natures that are hardened to evil you shall sooner break than make straight; they are like poles that are crooked and dry; there is no attempting them.
—Ben Jonson, *Timber*, vii (Dick Cheney)

And when your days go on
No one knows but you.
—The Gasoline Band, ★ "Loafers End"

"Geniuses have the shortest biographies" because their inner lives are led out of sight and earshot; and in the end "their cousins can tell you nothing about them."★
—Andrew Delbanco, quoting Emerson,
"The Great Leviathan," *NYRB*, May 15, 1997

The most challenging work on the first half [of the program] is the *Clair de lune*, which I try to play without a trace of metric freedom: Debussy has infused it with metric freedom; adding to it just takes it away.
—Nancy Garniez, program note for "Offbeat Beethoven"
recital, February 2014

What was the great objective behind 19th century liberalism? It was, as Marx never tired to point out, to separate the economic sphere from the political sphere and to confine politics to the latter while leaving the economic sphere to capital. . . . It is liberalism's splendid success in achieving this long-held goal that we are now observing.
—Yanis Varoufakis, Greek economist and minister of finance,
quoted in *The Case for Meritocracy*

On the Brooklyn Heights Library there is a panel that says, *All that come here to seek treasure will not take away gold but the seeker after truth and*

instruction will find that which will enrich the mind and heart. We will continue to protect libraries as places to enrich all minds and hearts and stop those who seek gold.
 —Carolyn McIntyre, co-founder of
  Citizens Defending Libraries

The unmaking of the world.

Late! It had only just got started!
 —Adam Thirlwell, on the era of Late Capitalism, *Lurid & Cute*

our common disaster
 —James Baldwin

Other poets have worked for the Water Bureau.
 —Su Tung-p'o, "On First Arriving at Huang-Chou,"
  trans. Burton Watson

When a drunken man falls from a carriage, though the carriage may be going very fast, he won't be killed ... because his spirit is whole. He didn't know he was riding, and he doesn't know he has fallen out.
 —Chuang Tzu, "The Full Understanding of Life"

The violist of the Beethoven Quartet was once given the following advice about the first movement of the fifteenth quartet by its composer [Shostakovich]: "Play it so that the flies drop dead in mid-air."
 —Julian Barnes, *Nothing to Be Frightened Of*

The Socratic aim is to reduce confidence, inducing disorientation, leading to *aporia*, a puzzled halt.

This piling up of maxims (*sententiae*) is something Quintilian condemned:

They make for a broken-up speech, since each maxim stands apart, and one must start over when each one ends. . . . Such neat and rounded maxims do not interconnect. . . . No matter how flashy each is on its own, they do not make a single conflagration, but separate sparks in a smoky haze, and they have no impact in a truly luminous speech, as the stars disappear in daylight.
—GARRY WILLS, *Rome and Rhetoric*

Act so there is no use in a center.
—GERTRUDE STEIN, "Rooms," *Tender Buttons*

Eddie Condon said Bix Beiderbecke's sound on cornet was "like a girl saying yes."

The musician is perhaps the most modest of animals, but he is also the proudest. It is he who invented the sublime art of ruining poetry.
—ERIK SATIE

"The thing is, you have to write the bad poems as well as the good ones."

Rilke: *That's the gods' business. It's up to them.*

Coptic paintings, textiles, and sculptures . . . speak to us in a voice which laughs at the gaps in our knowledge.
—DIKRAN KELEKIAN

In 1999, in a public conversation with William Ferris, chairman of the National Endowment for the Humanities, B. B. King recounted how he came to sing the blues:

"Growing up on the plantation there in Mississippi, I would work Monday through Saturday noon," he said. "I'd go to town on Saturday afternoons, sit on the street corner, and I'd sing and play."

"I'd have me a hat or box or something in front of me. People that would request a gospel song would always be very polite to me, and they'd say: 'Son, you're mighty good. Keep it up. You're going to be great one day.' But they never put anything in the hat.

"But people that would ask me to sing a blues song would always tip me and maybe give me a beer. They always would do something of that kind. Sometimes I'd make 50 or 60 dollars one Saturday afternoon. Now you know why I'm a blues singer."

We are never permitted to despair of the commonwealth.
—Thomas Jefferson, letter to James Madison,
December 20, 1787 (via George Scialabba)

Don't leave power on the table. Don't give it away.
—Zephyr Teachout, in an interview

Who shall guard the Guardians? Who shall censor the censors? The question is unanswerable without a theory of absolution. It is not answerable in a secular framework. There must be a class or caste of people outside society who are shunned or kept at a physical distance because they touch pollution. Hence the sweeper caste in India, hence the priestly caste in Gwope. Priests cannot marry because they are polluted/holy. That is why priests cannot sleep with decent women, cannot marry: they must sleep with whores. A para-priestly class like the SS (created to perform abominations) has brothels created for it: it is the idea of a domestic life for SS men that offends us most deeply.
    —J. M. COETZEE, *Age of Iron*

Fiction, being a serious affair, cannot accept pre-requisites like (1) a desire to write, (2) something to write about, (3) something to say. There must be a place for a fiction of apathy towards the task of writing, towards the subject, towards the means.
    —J. M. COETZEE, "The Burning of the Books"

In 1994 [Tabucchi] wrote a novel, *The Last Three Days of Fernando Pessoa*, in which a hospitalized Pessoa, who also practiced spiritualism and automatic writing, meets the main heteronyms he had invented and discusses life, death, and identity with them, always in the politest, most decorous terms. "The gods will return," says Pessoa at one point, quoting his imaginary mentor António Mora, "because this story of the single soul and only one god is a transient thing." Then "our souls can be plural again, as Nature desires."
    —TIM PARKS, *NYRB*, June 4, 2015

... but if we look to poetry as a skill by which we can grasp the form of a perception achieved ...
>—George Oppen, "Three Poets," *Selected Prose, Daybooks and Papers*

If Oehlen has a method, it is to recoil, stroke by stroke, from conventional elegance—strangling one aborning stylistic grace after another.
>—Peter Schjeldahl, "Painting's Point Man," *The New Yorker*, June 22, 2015

Painting isn't dead except as a major art. From now on it will be a discourse of adepts, like jazz.
>—Dave Hickey, quoted by Peter Schjeldahl, *The New Yorker*, June 22, 2015

... qualities that I want to see brought together: delicacy and coarseness, color and vagueness, and, underlying them all, a base note of hysteria.
>—Albert Oehlen, interview in the catalog for his show *Home and Garden* at the New Museum, quoted by Peter Schjeldahl, *The New Yorker*, June 22, 2015

I'm reminded of the scene in Jorge Semprún's memoirs, *Quel beau dimanche*. After his family was expelled from Spain, he, at the age of twenty, was swept into the French Resistance and subsequently arrested as a communist. Sent to Buchenwald, he was taken under the wing of an old German communist—which doubtless explains his survival. At one point Semprún asks the older man to explain "dialectics" to him. And the answer comes back: "C'est l'art et la manière de toujours retomber sur ses pattes, mon vieux"—the art and the technique of always landing on your feet. And so it is with rabbinical rhetorics: the art and the technique—above all the art—of landing on your feet in a solid position of authority and

conviction. To be a revolutionary Marxist was to make a virtue of your rootlessness, not least the absence of religious roots, while clinging—even if only half knowingly—to a style of reasoning which would have been very familiar to every Hebrew school student.
 —Tony Judt, *Thinking the Twentieth Century*

... Roland Barthes' lifelong uneasiness with competition, his mistrust of binary situations and his dreamy commitment to a third language in which we would all be exempt from meaning.
 —Anne Carson (Ashbery?)

I suppose that if I ever go to Paris the first person I meet will be myself since I have been there in one way or another for so long ...
 —Wallace Stevens, letter to Bernard Heringman,
  February 10, 1950

Me: "A poem should be as good as a cigarette or a drink."
David Rattray: "That's pretty *good!*"

This is one of the great enigmas of modern life: why the representation of a thing can fascinate those who would ignore the original.

... entertainment, that hybrid and ever-evolving mix of sophisticated technique and populist content.

What was being lost as the real thing was returning as imagery.

the *Cinématographe* (Lumière brothers, 1895)

the desire for the real
 —Rebecca Solnit, *River of Shadows*

Plato mistrusts poetry because it cannot be contained, meanings spill over, e.g., the sadism of his metaphor of the cave, like a machine out of Kafka.

You can make a fresh start with your final breath.
    —Brecht, "Everything Changes," via Joe Chaikin

Those who cannot let down their own trousers rule nations.
    —Brecht, *The Caucasian Chalk Circle*

Those who take the most from the table, teach contentment. Those for whom the taxes are destined, demand sacrifice. Those who eat their fill, speak to the hungry of wonderful times to come. Those who lead the country into the abyss, call ruling too difficult for ordinary folk.
    —Brecht, *A German War Primer*

What is robbing a bank compared to founding a bank?
    —Brecht, *The Threepenny Opera*

The Becks, according to Chaikin himself, have had the most profound influence on him of anyone. In 1967 he told me that he couldn't imagine what he would be like or what he would be thinking about if he hadn't worked with them. They led him to Brecht, to Artaud, and the poetic drama. They opened up his political and social conscience. They impressed him with their fanatical commitment to their work. They set him a model for the communal structure of theatre work and for the confrontation of one's life with the values which emerge from one's work. Their respect for persons and disrespect for institutions are in Chaikin, as well as their spirit of self-criticism. He is struck, as he wrote of them (*Village Voice*, October 17, 1968), by their demonstration "in their work and in their activism that there are almost no boundaries; that no one need stay within the

limitations which seem to be fixed. They represent a repudiation of the captive way of life. That is their spectacle."
    —Robert Pasolli, *A Book on the Open Theatre*

When Penelope Gilliatt mentioned Brecht's poems to Jean-Luc Godard, he replied, "They are optimistic when I am sad. They are written from a standpoint of not being certain, and it's a very good way to convince. They say that the world is not sad, it is big."

This is the god in whose body I walk
    —Beverly Dahlen, *The Egyptian*

Among the heaps of brick and plaster lies
a girder, still itself among the rubbish.
    —Charles Reznikoff, "Jerusalem the Golden," 69

The direction out from illusion is not up, at any rate not up to one fixed morning star; but down, at any rate along each chain of a day's denial. Philosophy (as descent) can thus be said to leave everything as it is because it is a refusal of, say disobedient to, (a false) ascent, or transcendence. Philosophy (as ascent) shows the violence that is to be refused (disobeyed), that has left everything not as it is, indifferent to me, as if there are things in themselves. Plato's sun has shown us the fact of our chains; but that sun was produced by these chains.
    —Stanley Cavell, *This New Yet Unapproachable America*

We are faced by a direct confrontation between the large transnational corporations and the states. The corporations are interfering in the fundamental political, economic and military decisions of the states. The corporations are global organizations that do not depend on any state and

whose activities are not controlled by, nor are they accountable to any parliament or any other institution representative of the collective interest. In short, all the world political structure is being undermined.
 —S%%ALVADOR%% A%%LLENDE%%, speech at the United Nations,
  December 4, 1972

The Environmental Protection Agency accused the German automaker of using software to detect when the car is undergoing its periodic state emissions testing. Only during such tests are the cars' full emissions control systems turned on. During normal driving situations, the controls are turned off, allowing the cars to spew as much as 40 times as much pollution as allowed under the Clean Air Act, the E.P.A. said.
 —*The New York Times*, September 19, 2015

. . . austerity, the Trojan Horse for dismantling labor rights and the welfare state.
 —M%%ARIA%% M%%ARGARONIS%%, *The Nation*, August 26, 2015

The poem as worksite: *Maximus*

love work that sails close
to its own parody
 —A%%NSELM%% H%%OLLO%%

I especially like the poem "Fragment" in the new book. I asked him a couple of weeks back what it was a fragment OF. "Just a fragment," he told me. "That's how it came out and that's how I left it."
 —A%%UGUST%% K%%LEINZAHLER%%, on Christopher Middleton

a will toward meaning
—William Kentridge

He learned a great deal from the company of John Wieners.
—Alan Davies, of himself

When I told the cardiologist I was seeing last spring that I was a poet he stopped what he was doing, threw up his hands, exclaimed "The heart!" and started talking to me as to a fellow specialist.

[The fossil fuel industry is] clearly willing to break the planet if it means five or perhaps ten more years of business as usual for them.
—Bill McKibben, *The Guardian*, December 13, 2015

We are no longer frightened of nature; what frightens us is the idea that we have triumphed over nature, and what that triumph will mean in the long run, when we understand, too late, that we *were* nature, that our triumph has been a suicide. . . . We believed all along that the thing we were fighting to dominate was at bottom unconquerable. Jefferson thought it would take a thousand years to populate the frontier. We did not know our own strength.
—John Jeremiah Sullivan, *Blood Horses*

[About Frank Kuenstler] Poets should take care of their own. Working on *The Enormous Chorus*, when I asked Bill Corbett "What are we going to do about Frank's long lines?", he said, without hesitation, "We won't break them." Likewise Jerry Rothenberg's simple assumption that it was self-evident that this book should exist.

A word about the title. He was large. The poems are very ambitious. There's a surface wit that makes them seem more casual than they are. "The Dream of a Common Language" and "Of Being Numerous" both offer ways of thinking about them. No one listened more intently.

He wouldn't let himself be stopped. No publisher? the copy shop, the post office, the edition of one. Typewriter broken, no lower case? solid caps, THE RABBI KYOTO POEMS. No film, maybe no camera? found footage, *El Atlantis*.

The world is more complicated than the truths about it.
    —STEFAN THEMERSON, *Wooff, Wooff*

On the first page of *Une Saison en enfer* Rimbaud says

Un soir, j'ai assis la Beauté sur mes genoux. —Et je l'ai trouvée amère. —Et je l'ai injuriée. ★

Toward the end of "Alchimie du Verbe" he says

Le Bonheur était ma fatalité, mon remords, mon ver: ma vie serait toujours trop immense pour être dévouée à la force et à la beauté. ★

But at the very end of "Alchimie du Verbe," after all the poems he's rejecting, he says

Cela s'est passé. Je sais aujourd'hui saluer la beauté. ★

So: What did he know? How *did* he salute beauty? with the *Illuminations*? with his silence? did he still care? I wish I could ask David Rattray, he might have known.

Imagination though it cannot wipe out the sting of remorse can instruct the mind in its proper uses.
　—WILLIAMS, *Kora in Hell*

Anybody not enlightened by a thunderbolt deserves respect.
　—BASHŌ

Jazz is "about freedom, beyond that it gets complicated."
　—THELONIOUS MONK

All films are about the theatre; there is no other subject.

There is no *auteur* in films . . . a film is something that preexists in its own right. It is only interesting if you have this feeling that the film preexists and that you are trying to reach it, to discover it, taking precautions to avoid spoiling it or deforming it.

Time was, in a so-called classical tradition of cinema, when the preparation of a film meant first of all finding a good story, developing it, scripting it and writing dialogue; with that done, you found actors who suited the characters and then you shot it. . . . What I have tried is to attempt to find, alone or in company . . . a generating principle that will then, as though on its own (I stress the "as though"), develop in an autonomous manner and engender a film product from which, afterwards, a film destined eventually for screening for audiences can be cut, or rather "produced."
　—JACQUES RIVETTE, interview, April 1973

[Noguchi] seems to have gotten away from the Western artist's concern about the place in the world of what he makes. His objects are his surroundings quite literally. There is no nonsense about use of objects because apparently in Japan art does not exist apart from life, but is a form, a ceremony of daily existence. He says of things that could be considered flat dishes, "sculpture may lie down." The vases do not have to have water in them, they do not have to contain grasses or flowers. There are frogs and centipedes and Japanese figures expressed in the terms required by the language of curved sheets of clay, that have an ease, grace and appreciation and respect for the earth, for the mineral as well as animal and human world that this reviewer has not seen in modern Western ceramic art, including Picasso. All the careful calculation that was needed in his stone carving has turned into something that, because it includes and admits and loves actuality instead of an ideal, has an elegance that is of the sort that is looked for in what passes for perfection.

... the school of de Kooning, which does something new in art. It takes as the subject matter for artistic contemplation, workmanship as such, good and bad, which is directly before the artist: the work, including the craft, of painting. It includes a contemplation of the work content of all art from the classics to modern advertising, and from skill of hand to the awkwardness of an amateur painting his boat in the spring. A spill, a blister of paint is as much part of the subject matter for artistic contemplation as the virtuosity of Frans Hals. Work is transformed into art.
    —FAIRFIELD PORTER

Which when her sad-beholding husband saw,
Amazedly in her sad face he stares.
Her eyes, though sod in tears, looked red and raw,
Her lively color killed with deadly cares.
He hath no power to ask her how she fares;
Both stood, like old acquaintance in a trance,
Met far from home, wond'ring each other's chance.
    —*The Rape of Lucrece*, ll. 1590–96

After researching the history and philosophy of American education, Swartz concluded that the system was working exactly as it was intended

to: inducing compliance and boredom in order to pre-empt future labor agitation, and teaching everyone very little in the process.
—Ava Kofman, "The Trials of Aaron Swartz,"
The Nation, February 3, 2016

My job, as I see it, has never been to lay a tit's egg, but to erupt like a volcano, emitting not only flame, but a lot of rubbish.
—Hugh MacDiarmid, letter to George Bruce, July 1, 1964

But one must remember that such vocabulary is often intended more to astound the reader than to convey to him a clear and comprehensible picture of what is going on.
—Burton Watson, *Chinese Rhyme-Prose*

Hölderlin ". . . prepared, as he wrote Böhlendorff on the eve of his departure [for Bordeaux], to lay himself open to the lightning (his chosen 'sign,' he explained, for the manifestation of the divine)."
—Richard Sieburth

"his chosen sign" . . . and René Char's

Instead of inventing riddles for prize students, he scattered about his pages a number of pregnant passages containing all the clues that are needed for keeping up with him.
—Theodora Bosanquet, "Henry James at Work"

But he knows that these things happen, not in the real world and not in the world of fantasy, but in another world.
Of a poet: "something about his writing that was bright (i.e., sun-drenched) and full of hope."
—Yoel Hoffmann, *Bernhard*

> . . . O wirst du dies Motiv
> erfinden noch, eh sich dein Lied verzehrte?★
> —Rilke, *Sonnets to Orpheus* I, 2 (speaking to Fred Schwartz★)

> Doricha, your bones are adorned by the ribbon tying your soft tresses
> and by the perfumed shawl
> in which once you wrapped the handsome Charaxus,
> flesh against flesh, until the morning cup.
> But the white, echoing pages of Sappho's song
> remain and will live on.
> Most blessed is your name, and Naucratis will watch over it
> so long as ships pass by on the still Nile, heading seaward.
> —Posidippus, in Roberto Calasso's
>   *Marriage of Cadmus and Harmony*

> Aha Is it in / out of this other world that a poem can say with certainty and unassailable credibility "dreaming of horses"?
> —Allen Brafman

> How many, think ye, have likewise fallen into Plato's honey head, and sweetly perished there?
> —*Moby-Dick*, chapter 78

> Ashbery wrote that he and O'Hara "felt that art is already serious enough; there is no point in making it seem even more serious by taking it too seriously."
> —Jenni Quilter, "The Real Thing," *LRB*, April 21, 2016

> Literature: How many unpleasant traits did people ascribe to you, as if you were a flighty woman who thinks of nothing but new clothes? Will you still sometimes open your door to the being that no longer frequents

philosophy texts, that lies wordless among the algorithms?
—Roberto Calasso, "Wake for Montaigne," *The Ruin of Kasch*

un vieux, dragueur, dans sa barque immobile, peine.*
—Rimbaud, "Mémoire"

Freud, for example, described the long and circuitous path to so-called normal femininity for the girl—originally bisexual, wildly energised by being all over the place—as nothing short of a catastrophe.
—Jacqueline Rose, "Who do you think you are?"
LRB, May 5, 2016

Our lynching-picnic roots have been showing a long time. Revolution may not be in the offing, but social suicide is possible. In such a situation, where being offensive is the dominant theme of cultural and political life, to offend is not radical, any more than murder is. Where everything is irreverence, reverence is the resistant act—for ourselves, for the integrity of another human soul, for the connections that bind us, in possibility and peril.
—JoAnn Wypijewski, "Night Thoughts," *The Nation*, April 6, 2015

Flaubert's "Ils sont dans le vrai": "They have it right"

... because we felt the futility of peaceful words without peaceful deeds.
—Daniel Berrigan

Whoever expects a "pure" social revolution will never live to see it.
—Lenin, on Easter 1916,
"The Discussion on Self-Determination Summed Up,"

The Someone that he is guilty before is not a stern god, a father, but his living deprived Self, not cut off from desire and suffering anxiety.
  —Paul Goodman, *Kafka's Prayer*

The bounded is loathed by its possessor. The same dull round, even of a universe, would soon become a mill with complicated wheels.
  —Blake, *There is No Natural Religion*

I have outlived my mission, and know no more of it.

I will wander the earth, and say nothing. For nothing is so marvelous as to be alone in the phenomenal world, which is raging, and yet apart.
  —D. H. Lawrence, *The Man Who Died*
    (the second noted by Charles Olson)

Do you realize that I am working obstinately and tenaciously with my brain, and am often in the best sense active when I present the appearance of a heedless and out-of-work, negligent, dreamy, and idle pickpocket, lost out in the blue, or in the green, making the worst impression, seeming a frivolous man devoid of any sense of responsibility?
  —Robert Walser, "The Walk"

Ethics does not treat of the world. Ethics must be a condition of the world, like logic.
  —Wittgenstein, *Notebooks*, July 24, 1916

Ó Riada told people that one should listen to *sean-nós* song either as a child would listen or as if they were songs from India.
  —*Wikipedia*

I remember what Agnés Varda said to me: "I hope you make us a good film because we all love that book."
—Michel Gondry (the book is Boris Vian's *L'Écume des jours*)

The stargazers of old had a nice formulation whereby they spoke of this or that theory of the heavens "saving the phenomena": that is, agreeing with what was to be observed of planetary motions, but not necessarily claiming to be a direct representation of what actually happens out there in those infinite spaces the thought of which so disturbed Pascal's peace of mind."
—John Banville, "What have clocks got to do with it?"
   LRB, July 14, 2016

The composer will know that he is one if composition creates exact appetites in him, and if in satisfying them he is aware of their exact limits.
—Stravinsky, in Robert Craft, *Conversations with Igor Stravinsky*

Perhaps every child's animistic view of the unknown world which they unaccompanied must enter fearfully, is the truest view of our world and the cosmos at large which we are likely to be vouchsafed?
—Aidan Higgins, *A Bestiary*

Perhaps what cannot be said is the ground on which what can be said comes by its meaning.

Time is the empty house that being inhabits.
—Guy Davenport, "The Death of Picasso"

Notes and Translations

Page 1
Oh, how picturesque, missed trains! . . .

How they sound: "See you soon! See you soon!"
The boats
At the end of the pier . . .
Of the well-made pier.
Against the sea,
Like my flesh
Against love.
   —Jules Laforgue, *Last Poems*, x

Page 2
Inert, everything burns . . .
   —Mallarmé, "The Afternoon of a Faun"

Page 3
He laughed at me when he saw me studying Greek at the age of twenty: "You are on the field of battle," he said, "it is no longer the time to polish your rifle; you must shoot."
   —Prosper Mérimée, *Stendhal*

Page 4
Joan Farber, artist, Michael's wife

Page 6
I would like my old sorrows to be like the gravel in the river: at the bottom. My currents would not care.
   —René Char, "Spice Hunters"

Page 13
If we dwell in a flash of lightning, it is the heart of the eternal.
   —René Char, "To the Health of the Snake"

Page 14
Cf. *Loquitur*, Basil Bunting's 1965 book of poems

Page 17
SALLY GROSS, dancer, choreographer, Michael's tai chi instructor

Page 20
"G." Michael may be referring to Gustaf Sobin

Page 20
DICK MULLIKEN, friend of Michael and Joan's from Delaware County, New York

Page 21
RACHELLE GARNIEZ, singer, songwriter, old friend of Michael's

Page 27
The important thing is not to heal but to live well with one's ills.
  —L'ABBÉ GALIANI, via Ned Rorem

Page 27
SUSAN BUTLER, photographer, friend of Michael's

Page 31
PEGUY. Geoffrey Hill uses this passage as the epigraph to *The Mystery of the Charity of Charles Peguy*, where it is quoted in French.

Page 36
But is there a poetry open to reality and a poetry closed on words?
  —RENÉ NELLI, *Poetry Open Poetry Closed*

Page 39
The gods give everything, the infinite ones,
To their darlings completely:

Every joy, the infinite ones,
Every pain, the infinite ones, completely.
 —GOETHE, in Kafka, *Diaries*, 1912

Page 40
SIDEWALK. This is a translation of a haiku by Ryokan (1758-1831).

Page 42
and what are poets for in destitute times?
 —HÖLDERLIN, "Bread and Wine"

Page 44
Another one of my dead pierrots;
Dead of a chronic orphancy;
His was a heart full of moony
Dandyism in so odd a body.
 —JULES LAFORGUE, "Locutions of Pierrot," xii

Page 45
DENNIS/SWIFT. The full quote, from Swift's April 20, 1731 letter to Alexander Pope, reads: *The common saying of life being a farce is true in every sense but the most important one, for it is a ridiculous tragedy, which is the worst kind of composition.*

Page 53
BARBARA GREENBERG, artist, old friend of Michael's

Page 58
JOYCE. I'm at the end of English.

Page 61
LEVIN. Thackeray says it in *The English Humorists of the Eighteenth Century*.

Page 70
>	Tree Struck by Lightning
>		I.
> The vast thunderbolt and the fire of its kiss
> Beguile my tomb that the tempest built.
>
>		II.
> Snatched by the bird of scattered sorrow
> And dropped in the woods as a labor of love.
>	—René Char, trans. Bill Zavatsky and Mark Polizzotti

Page 71
Allen Brafman, poet, old friend of Michael's

Page 82
Mike Eigen, psychoanalyst

Page 92
Ellis Cooper, professor of mathematics, old friend of Michael's

Page 100
> Simplicity even to write
> For today the hand is there.
>	—Paul Éluard, "Confections"

Page 108
> ...the room where I came to break with you the bread of our desires
>	—Paul Éluard, "Shared Nights"

Page 116
Char/"To abolish..." From L'Âge cassant [The Brittle Age], translated by Gustaf Sobin.

Page 132
MONTAIGNE/BLOOM. The Montaigne quote, from "Of Physiognomy," reads: *If you don't know how to die, don't worry; Nature will tell you what to do on the spot, fully and adequately. She will do this job perfectly for you; don't bother your head about it.*

Page 135
JACK. Possibly John Unterecker

Page 136
There is surely another world, but it is in this one.
  —PAUL ÉLUARD

Page 140
There is nothing in the intellect which is not first in the senses.
  —AQUINAS

Page 141
WILLS/CHESTERTON. The Chesterton quote is found in *Orthodoxy*: *[Democracy] is, on the contrary, a thing analogous to writing one's own love-letters or blowing one's own nose. These things we want a man to do for himself, even if he does them badly.*

Page 141
The poem is a furious ascent; poetry, a game on arid embankments.
  —RENÉ CHAR, *Leaves of Hypnos*

Page 143
The poet is a mason, he arranges stones; the prose writer mixes and pours concrete.
  —PIERRE REVERDY, *My Logbook*

Page 149
NANCY GARNIEZ, pianist, music theorist, old friend of Michael's

Page 151
GASOLINE BAND. A '60s rock group, of which Michael's friend Fred Schwartz was keyboard man and composer.

Page 151
DELBANCO/EMERSON. The Emerson quote, found in "Plato, or the Philosopher," reads: *Great geniuses have the shortest biographies. Their cousins can tell you nothing about them.*

Page 162
One evening I sat Beauty on my lap. And I found her bitter. And I insulted her.

Happiness was my fatality, my remorse, my worm: my life would always be too immense to be devoted to strength and beauty.

That's finished. Today I know how to greet beauty.
 —RIMBAUD

Page 166
             Ah will you discover
this theme before your song consumes itself?
 —RILKE, *Sonnets to Orpheus* I, 2

FRED SCHWARTZ, pianist, composer, old friend of Michael's

Page 167
an old man, a dredger, in his motionless boat, labors.
 —RIMBAUD, "Memory"

MICHAEL O'BRIEN (1939–2016) was born and raised in Granville, New York, and lived thereafter in New York City; studied at Fordham, the University of Paris, and Columbia; worked as a librarian; was one of the Eventorium poets, where his first book was published in 1967; taught at Brooklyn College and Hunter; worked for many years editing technical publications; wrote *The Summer Poems, Conversations at the West End, Blue Springs, Veil, Hard Rain, The Floor and the Breath, Seventeen Songs, Sills: Selected Poems 1960–1999, Six Poems, Sleeping and Waking, Avenue,* and *To the River.*

www.ingramcontent.com/pod-product-compliance
Lightning Source LLC
Chambersburg PA
CBHW031110080526
44587CB00011B/910